Leabharlann Ráth Eanaigh
Raheny Library
01-2228323

THE STATE OF DARK

JUDITH MOK

'*The State of Dark* is a privilege to read. With luminous prose, Judith Mok shines a light into the darkness of her family's past. It is an extraordinary feat of storytelling to be able to write about inconceivable tragedies with such warmth and humanity.'

LOUISE NEALON

'At this particular point in history with the rise of authoritarian regimes, this crucially important book reminds us of how it went last time.

'Filled with music, poetry, love, friendship and horror, the history of Judith Mok's family is a testament to survival against all the odds. Courageous, brutally honest and uniquely profound, you will find nothing else like it on bookshelves this year. F

D1439773

For Them

THE STATE OF DARK
JUDITH MOK

THE LILLIPUT PRESS

First published 2022 by
THE LILLIPUT PRESS
62–63 Arbour Hill
Dublin 7, Ireland
www.lilliputpress.ie

Text copyright © Judith Mok, 2022

All rights reserved. No part of this publication may be reproduced in any form or by any means without prior permission of the publisher.

A CIP record for this publication is available from The British Library.

10 9 8 7 6 5 4 3 2 1

ISBN 978 1 84351 8501

The Lilliput Press gratefully acknowledges the financial support of the Arts Council/An Chomhairle Ealaíon.

Set in 10pt on 15pt Sabon LT Pro by Niall McCormack.
Printed in Spain by GraphyCems.

CONTENTS

Illustrations fall between pages 58 and 59.

ACKNOWLEDGMENTS

First and foremost I would like to thank my husband the author Michael O'Loughlin for helping me with this book. As an editor, as an extremely inspirational and knowledgeable advisor, and as a friend. My daughter Saar who was always ready to help and support.

Professor Clíona Ní Ríordáin for her encouragement, her time and her very much appreciated advice. Marina Guinness for her support, enthusiasm and appreciation of my work. Glen Hansard and author Maire Saaritsa, who supported my work and efforts during the recent difficult Covid years. Kevin Brew for his patience, and understanding of my work. Lisa Phillips, who introduced me to several quintessential readers in New York.

My parents, who gave me the strength to be able to write this book about them. Nora Hickey M'Sichili and the Centre Culturel Irlandais Paris, who offered me the space and peace to work. The people at the office of the Westerbork transit camp who provided me with information. Ellius Grace for his indispensable help with the photographs. Marc van Meurs for the Amsterdam photographs.

Thanks to all at The Lilliput Press for their hard work and dedication to this book.

DUBLIN 2017

SHE IS TALKING to me on the phone. She is sick, she says, but the doctors are giving her the right treatment. She is old, she says. But to me her voice sounds young, like a child speaking from inside an older woman. 'I was there,' she says. Again the smothered voice of a guilty child, stumbling over her words to hide the truth: 'I never told you.'

Where to begin?

I have carried this story with me to so many countries and cities, I, Judith Mok, musician, writer, wanderer. When I look in a mirror I see the reflection of a woman with the features of her parents clearly defined in her face. The face of someone belonging to a second generation, the children born and brought up by a first generation who had been left on their own, who had managed to survive all attempts on their lives by a regime that meant to exterminate them like vermin. And there in the mirror again, I am struck by the disturbing and maybe morbidly comical thought that regularly occurs to me: is this what human vermin look like?

We must have done so to a large group of people, people that I would still consider to be human beings, just like me. Why would I consider those people as human beings? Because of the way in which I have been brought up. By parents who made the songs and books and the many languages they mastered be our family. We learned to lean on knowledge for support, to admire and cultivate feelings for all sorts of art forms and intellectual inventions and endeavours. With great love and care they built us an existence and a world that could be relied on. The unbearable memories, the ghosts of those who had

Leabharlanna Poiblí Chathair Baile Átha Cliath
Dublin City Public Libraries

shared their warmth by simply existing as their family, were stuck in a time warp, they were rarely spoken of.

There were some rescued photographs, some stories told or songs sung under trees, trees that I would always associate with the past of my family and their friends. There were some objects that were of a mysterious significance to us children.

There was this theatre in Amsterdam which made me, as a professional performer, realize from the beginning of my performing career how thin the dividing line between the different functionalities of buildings can be: one day a stage, next day a prison, next decade, a monument.

And there was the phonebook. The phonebook with all the invisible rows of missing names. Year after year my father would open it and stare at the pages as if in disbelief. The authorities must have made a mistake. He knew the truth, but always looked for proof.

A LETTER TO MY DAUGHTER

MY DEAREST CHILD, *my darling Saar. I gave you that name because of her, your great-aunt Saar. As far as I know you have never seen a photograph of her ...*

... I did what my parents avoided doing during the fairly short time I shared with them: I looked back. I realize how hard it must have been for them to show the kindness they had in them. Their love was all important to me. It is what went missing, what is behind those times, that I want to tell you about. I wrote about their world and I tried to describe the seasons of their lives to you.

This is my wall. I constructed it with a number of markings in my notebook: for every murdered soul, a small stripe, a blood brick in my existence. This is the wall that they, your grandparents, are now on the other side of.

A State of Dark exists beyond that wall. From any belief in tikkun olam, *all they held onto were the shards of the forever shattered light. They put together an existence so new that there was no room for a mere shadow.*

Every time in our existence that we, their children, are intent on making, living or loving, we have to take the wall into consideration. What it hides, what does not exist, is what we base our lives on now.

We don't know how to ride camels, like semites from a distant desert time, any more than we know how to dance in wooden clogs just because we assimilated into the culture of a country called Holland. What we believe in are their, our parents', memories. Nothing else. We learned that every life has its worth and yet, behind that wall, it was worthless. The tightly organized energy of destruction and death stands like a giant looking over at us from behind that wall. It reached out to me through the work of my father and that of many other great artists.

There is no scale of things to consider, no lead to follow through a labyrinth of centuries. There is no way to approach the scattered pieces of the puzzle, no way to make it whole again. There is the monumentally raised possiblity of the acceptance of absurdity; a frozen balance to live with, almost like some seperate being. We, now, move ourselves through life, away or close to the wall, aware of the State of Dark.

Not a single war can be won.

Remember: they, those left behind, lost that war. They lost the hands that broke the bread, and had to live by bread alone.

And here you are.

In my Dublin home I talk to my reflection in the mirror about the letter I just wrote to my daughter.

I mentioned *tikkum olam,* repairing the world with kindness it is said to mean in Hebrew these days. Bringing back the shattered light was the ancient rabinnic meaning. Making the world whole again. Shards of light, shards of mirror. Each shard of my reflection in this mirror contains my memories of them and how I would like to bring them back to the light.

MOTHER: RINGS OF SMOKE

MOTHER, I LOVED watching you smoke – slow to inhale, slow to exhale – your breath in rings in the light. Your hands with the simple silver ornaments on your fingers, fingers that grew knotted with time, as some trees do. One hand resting on the open page of a book, the other somewhere mid-air, holding the cigarette, the little glowing at the end that marked your hours. Never more than five to seven a day, you said. Cigarettes. I never touched them, my sister never touched them. In our family, maybe they were only meant for you. Smoking was an ordinary thing to do and, like all children, I liked you being ordinary. Although, once, I caught you out as extraordinary at the hairdresser's, your short, wet hair combed back, the hairdresser holding up his scissors behind you like an executioner and you smoking in the mirror in front of you. Your face already carved by age and your smoking, that had developed to a stage of smooth sophistication.

From my walk along the Delft canals, I had entered a hairdresser's salon where I found you, mother, incarnating an old-style Hollywood star, smoking. Suddenly you were that different person, the woman comfortable in her worldliness and the vast luxury of her knowledge. A woman who managed to overcome the war in her life, facing her own beautiful reflection for the time of one cigarette smoked with lascivious indulgence.

Otherwise, your smoking habits were like a roster to me. Early in the morning you made sure we were fed, and wrapped up if snow or storms hit the big windows of our living room. We cycled to school or you drove us through the dunes in our old car, again, depending on the weather. Once you had left us at the gates of our school I stopped thinking of you as the mother who had made my favourite sandwiches for lunch. I would sit in my classroom and during our first break, towards 10:30, I liked to think of you as the woman who started the rhythm of your own routine by sitting down and smoking her first cigarette of that day.

You smoked that cigarette talking to my father over a cup of coffee. Once he had closed his door, you sat down behind your desk with the light shining on your left hand through the remaining smoke and you started working on your newspaper column. The subject would be set in your mind by then. After a shared lunch for two, a second cigarette to mark the beginning of the afternoon, the french doors open, the last of the smoke often torn away by rough weather. Then a nap, a book, a walk, a friend's visit. The grocer or the milkman at the door, a thought about our daily food. Another cigarette mixed with the taste of your favoured tea, lapsang souchong, a walk along the beach, or a ride to our school to pick us up. The smoke we shared at half past five with cocktails and talking, with pickles and nuts while doing our homework before dinner. When I was in my bed, with the sea rolling in and out of my slumber, I sometimes thought I could hear you smoke your last cigarette of the day.

Did you learn all these poems, these wonderful words, by heart in the fluid rythm of your smoking? You visited me in Paris and in Barcelona, reciting the words of great poets like Mandelstam, Blok, Akhmatova, settled in smoke, and I listened, entranced. You packed the same, small suitcase so carefully that it hurt me to watch you spread a scarf over each layer of clothing or shoes. Then on top, a package of cigarettes.

Was your smoking habit there to hold on to something you had always done, long before the war? Of course there was no tobacco anymore then. During that irregular time of your life. After that time, you took it up again.

This smoking of yours was never an addiction, you could leave it aside when told that you were too sick to smoke and pick it up again when healed. It was a ritual that made me realize that you could organize your thoughts around your own time. Your hours passed through rings of smoke. ˍ

Father. I was not aware that I danced in and out of your work; that when you pulled me along the snow-covered beach on our green sleigh, with nothing said between us and nothing heard but the raw screeching of the seagulls, I was there in a new poem. I am still here. I do not want to move away from where you placed me.

The proud Spanish that I heard you speak when you were with the Chilean refugees, poets and writers all, or in long conversations with the Mexicans. The scribes who travelled with you on your reading trips.

But then, when you were old, in Barcelona where you came to live with me for a while, I went with you to buy a woollen cardigan. You said you were cold and you could not remember any Spanish. All the way to the little shop you were quoting lines of poems by the poets Machado, Lorca and Guillén in Spanish, but you did not know anymore how to buy a woollen garment. You, a descendant of Baruch ben Ishac ibn Daud, a Spanish Grandee and a Jew from Cordoba, disappeared behind a frayed curtain where a gas stove was burning, shivering and with your shoulders hunched, and I panicked. Where were they taking you, what was that tailor doing to you? You came out from behind that curtain soon enough, stroking the wool of a boring-looking beige cardigan, smiling broadly. You said your father used to have one just like it. You liked the quality of the wool. I wondered if Baruch ben Ishac ibn Daud, known as Don Bartolome, had worn a woollen cardigan in the ninth century in Andalusia, on a cold day, staring out over the mountains of the Sierra Nevada. You said he probably did, one of the finest lambswool. There was still a thread that held us together then. We all laughed, even the little tailor, who suddenly seemed very comfortable around my parents and me. I forgot that you had forgotten your Spanish.

You forgot so much more after that. You lost the iron routine, the timelines of your discipline, with which you wrote and translated philosophers. Adorno, Kant, Hegel, Sartre, all found their way into the Dutch language through you. In the mornings between breakfast and lunch you worked on them. In the afternoon you wrote your own words and walked them every day along the pristine beach of Bergen aan Zee or along the stretch of blue sea and sky in Menton, or along the canals of Amsterdam and Delft. I sometimes met you on these walks and you did not know me. I never minded this. I saw you were behind your iron bars of discipline, inside the bastion that kept you safe.

There is no horizon, you always said. In the Dutch landscape there is a land and a sky that never end. You liked that. A motherland and another horizon might have existed, behind this one, when you watched the sun go down in your daughter's garden, in a flat polder.

Your dreams were built on ashes, but you were grounded in them and you grew a new life for yourself, for your wife, for your children.

One summer day, back in Holland, I watched you potter around the garden, your frail body nearly transparent, carrying your ethereal crown of silver hair. Bent towards the ground, hesitant about coming across so much luscious fruit and greenery. The earth abundant, within your reach, you paced backwards and forwards for an hour. Then you sat down and you looked at me with tenderness in your eyes. I looked up at the unforgiving sky and down at the powerless ground.

You were eighty years old and now you wanted to go there. Behind the horizon.

Where did they go? you asked in so many of your poems. And then you asked me that same question, as I was sitting there, a woman in her early twenties dressed in a leopard print dress and pink spiky heels amongst the sprouting vegetables and the gooseberry bushes.

I, who had just uprooted myself out of a first marriage and had travelled back to my native country with nothing but my voice and a bundle of poems. I could not help you, although you told me then that you had chosen me to do so.

After that day, you spoke less, you did not write or read any more and you confused all the worlds that you lived in. Four months later your body went quietly. According to the Jewish tradition, we – your children and your wife – were not allowed to see you dead. Your soul had left your body. You were gone.

DUBLIN 2017

IT IS AN ONLINE phonebook that directs me towards the offices of what once used to be the Westerbork transit camp in Holland. A camp built in 1939 by the Dutch government to house the endless flow of Jewish immigrants, before it decided to close the borders. In 1940 the Germans occupied Holland and took over the camp to facilitate the transportation of the tens of thousands of Dutch Jews they would intern there to German concentration camps.

I have decided the time has come when I need to know what happened to my paternal grandparents and my aunt Saar. There was never enough courage in our family to rip down the curtain completely and face some naked facts. Facts that remain: date, year, the number of the barracks, train, camp, tattoo number, death.

On this bright day, the Dublin mountains are lit up by a soft sunlight. All is quiet, a cat hides behind my computer screen basking in its warm blast as I dial the number of the offices, still in place, of the former Westerbork camp and hold the phone to my ear. I pretend to myself that I just have to ask a practical question about some family history.

A very kind lady answers the phone. I explain who I am and what I am looking for. I wait for her to go through various computer files while I stare patiently out of the window. Yes, she says in that calm voice, there they were. The three of them arrived on 3 April, were put in prison barracks number 6 because they had been in hiding and were being punished. Then they were put on a transport train to Auschwitz on 7 April 1944.

My grandparents never got a tattoo number, she says. They went straight to the gas chambers when they got off the train.

With devastating speed, time has pulled me back to April 1944. I am still holding the phone with a shaking hand and, as tears start streaming down my face, I can see myself sitting in the space of a cold fact. My room has faded, my life has faded. Now I am the family member who knows exactly what happened to them, my close relatives. I try to find my voice, thanking the kind lady who must by now be used to her thankless task of telling the horrible truth. I also understand suddenly why my father did not get any details about his parents' deaths, whether they were gone or not; they didn't get a number and slipped through the mesh of the well-organized German administration. I talk and the lady agrees with me. She has something to add though. Would I like to get an email with a list of all the disappeared family members? I don't understand what she's saying, the landscape outside is blurry, my head is swimming. I stammer 'alright', and hang up to open my email.

While I sit reading, nailed to my chair, rows and rows of names appear on my screen; all these family members. Babies, teenagers, aunts, uncles, cousins.

My notebook is open and I start making a small mark on a blank page for each person that died. Sobibor, Auschwitz, Mauthausen, Trobitz, Treblinka. I count 163. Checking and checking again through unstoppable tears. I get up to wash my face and look up in the bathroom mirror only to see myself again, and again ask myself: why?

I sit down on my bed and unconciously stroke my grandfather Hijman's tallit, the prayer shawl he should have been buried in. Instead, it had been smuggled through the war by my father and is now covering the end of my bed. Only now do I realize that it might be time for me to speak where my parents stayed *stumm*, in order to let their new, post-war life take over. The silence they carried around with them was filled to the brim with dead voices. I read my father's extensive literary work and I listened to my mother's stories, but they passed on this terrible silence to me.

Why speak, why tell the tale told so many times already by great writers or courageous survivors? I ask myself this, feeling completly flat and empty.

It is because my parents' war wounds were so thinly healed that revealing them would have, without a doubt, killed them. Because everything they loved and stood for in their life and culture, had been destroyed in order to reduce them to barbarians themselves. Because, using their strength to try and convince us of the importance of an open, free and deep understanding of life, they had pushed away what they missed.

Also, because they and their families, had brought so much to their country. A richness in culture and love that took just a few minutes to wipe out. The scratchmarks of nails on the filthy wall of a Nazi gas chamber were supposed to be their legacy. Instead, I have to believe, that they would have liked for me to write their testament.

VIENNA 1979

THAT NIGHT THE train for Vienna leaves at eleven o'clock from Amsterdam Central Station. We arrive early to have a drink in the waiting room. It still has all the features of when it was first designed and built. This was the place where a close friend of my mother's would often meet up with her to encourage her to develop her talents as an actress, the place where he gave her presents of books, a first edition of Baudelaire's *Les Fleurs du Mal* for example, that he thought would inspire her.

I had been living in Paris for the previous two years and this was my first visit to the capital of what once was the great Austro-Hungarian Empire, a city where I was going to study with one of the great stars of the classical singing world, whom I had already worked with in Paris.

Though I was used to our goodbyes on the platform, I always found it hard to tear myself away from my parents' warmth, from their well-meant recommendations.

When we were in our late teens, my parents encouraged us to go and explore parts of Europe that they considered safe. We travelled, and had the use of the languages we had learned at home so not to feel helpless or misunderstood abroad. While I enjoyed interpreting for the friends who came with us, I also started to feel this growing sense of rootlessness. My friends talked about their homes and their countries as places where they were anchored. I was not familiar with those feelings. Though I felt secure and comfortable in my young independence, an equally strong feeling of melancholy started to settle in me.

My parents' waving hands and fading smiles, their growing older and smaller on the platform, and me settled in my train seat to go and live in yet another language. It soon became a pattern of my young life. I knew that those two beacons on the platform would inevitably become a memory. They were well into middle age when I was born, and death would catch up with them, leaving me to build on new beacons in my wanderer's life.

I was twenty-two when I arrived in Vienna, on a fresh morning. For a couple of nights I was housed in a home for young ladies, before I was to move in with a singer friend. The frills and dark colours of a conservative Austrian house were a little overpowering and, after leaving my two heavy suitcases in my room, I made for the streets. I was aware of the past of the country. How often had I been told that, though in Germany there were many people who refused to vote for Hitler, in Austria the tyrant had been received by an almost unanimously adoring population.

None of this was on my mind when I strolled to the Naschmarkt and inhaled the scents of herbs and vegetables completly unknown to me. A blanket of voices speaking, or rather shouting, in unfamiliar dialects and languages, spread in the air. It drifted over me, thick with wood and coal smoke. Chestnuts and sausages were being roasted by women, their heads bound with radiant scarves. When I looked up at the suns painted on the houses designed by the architect Wagner, men with broad shining faces winked at me. I told myself I had landed in a feast, close to where the musicians Mozart, Schubert and Mahler had lived and composed, close to where Freud had practiced his psychiatry, close to the cafés where artists and writers like Schiele, Schnitzler and Klimt (with his many women) had gathered for their lively discussions. Feeling dizzy with the mix of culture on offer I went and sat in one of those Viennese cafés that serve chocolate cakes, and sausages with freshly grated horseradish. Little did it matter that everybody around me was, or looked, stale and old, I had arrived in a city that used to have a great future.

At the home for young ladies I met the daughter of a train driver. She invited me to join her at her parents' house over the weekend. They lived near the Czech border. I had trouble understanding her parents' German and felt out of place eating the heavy food that they so kindly served. After dinner, the girl offered to walk me to the border, to see the posts, high up, where the soldiers stood watch with their rifles, to see where the barbed, electrified wire cut through the wild flowers in the field. Nobody could leave that country, she said. Her father told stories of train trips he had made. How he drove the train with the people who were allowed to leave Moscow to come to Vienna and then travel on. These were the Jewish people from Russia who, after many years of being prohibited from leaving the country, had finally been allowed travel visas to leave Russia and go to settle in Israel or, as was often the case, go straight to America. I should go, he said, early some morning to the Südbahnhof to see those bunches of families arrive.

I stayed the night and rushed back to Vienna the next day, to move out of the home and join my friends in their new apartment.

For a couple of months music takes over. I share the apartment with three other people. We set off to explore the mountains close to Vienna, we dance around at harvest feasts and we sit down some evenings to sight-read vocal quartets. We get tipsy on young wine and one night when we go to the theatre, I try to reproduce an image of myself as the *Judith* from Gustav Klimt's famous painting. We are young and we laugh and discuss all sorts of topics. Never the war, though.

It gets colder and snow starts to fall on Vienna. I schlep through the snow to the train that takes me to the suburbs where my teacher lives in her mansion. Struggling with my heavy boots and coat, I'm feeling a little sorry for myself on the long walk from the station to her place for my hour-long coaching session.

In her warm house, she laughs her tinkling singer's laugh at my frozen face, and says I should take the train from the Südbahnhof, it's a much shorter train ride to her suburb. I shake the snow off my clothes and shoes and suddenly remember that the train driver had mentioned this station. I felt as if a cold hand had gripped me by the throat at the idea of going to that station early in the morning. Now that it is mentioned again, it may be time to go have a look there though. A composer–conductor walks into my lesson to talk to my teacher. We shake hands and I am distracted from thoughts about the Südbahnhof until my lesson is over and I have to face the dark and the snow-schlep again. Ignoring my student budget I ask the housekeeper to call me a taxi. All the way back to my apartment.

When I tell my housemates that I plan to get up at five the next morning to see the emigrant trains from Russia arrive, my singer friend is dismissive. Her brother wants to know why. With wine to drink and a roaring stove, as if to smooth out the subject of our conversation a bit, we discuss the quite recent past of their country. My friend goes to bed, her brother and I talk through the night until it is time for me to go to the Südbahnhof.

At seven in the morning I am looking up at the soot-covered roof of the Südbahnhof, feeling warm in my coat and chewing on a *handsemmel*, a freshly baked roll. I don't know exactly why I seem to have followed myself to this place. The building was constructed around 1840 and nothing much seems to have been done to it since. Even the crows that are picking at invisible bits of food on the cracked platform seem more ancient and blacker than any I have ever seen. There are hardly any trains coming in from, or going out into, this dark winter morning. Melted snow drips on empty carriages, porters rattle their carts in expectation of a load. This is an end station, a terminus. No train can rush through to make you dream, in the moment it whooshes by, of undiscovered destinations.

Slowly the snow- and dirt-covered train enters the station. Dusty windows: no faces or movement noticable inside the compartments. But when the doors finally open entire families burst onto the platform where I stand waiting, and I suddenly feel a lightness in my head and a heartbeat in my stomach, as if I am expecting to meet people I have not seen in a long time, people close to me. Nobody notices me. They're dressed in rough wool and hard shoes, pushing and pulling at their badly tied-up luggage, their small children have faces swollen from tiredness. They all move as fast as they can towards the buses that will bring them to the airport, to freedom in the United States or Israel. Did I think the ones I had heard so much about would come back? Why this irrational feeling of excitement when I know that most of those people would be dead by now anyway, even if they had survived. Or was I just hoping for a joyous crowd of travellers that maybe would greet me on their way to a better future? Not this grey mass of humans who look as if they have had to dig themselves out of prison and who are rushing with bitter determination towards the unknown. When the crows resume their picking, I wander out of there. Back to music.

WHERE I STARTED

ON A LATE summer night two men, standing on a sand dune in Bergen aan Zee overlooking the North Sea, lifted their small glasses of jenever to the moon, and smiled at each other.

My mother, for she was my mother now that she had given birth to me, heard the men laugh from across the street. A warm wind blew through the marram grass into the open bedroom window and my mother said my name for the first time. Judith.

She chose my name as my father had chosen my older sister Marianne's name. Our doctor had assisted at my birth at home, in our house built on another sand dune. Even before my mother held me, he took me in his arms. My little bald head rested against the tattooed number on his arm, but nobody seemed to pay any attention to this fact.

The men were laughing because a new life, it just happened to be mine, had started and there were so many other reasons to laugh at life in general.

My mother who had been told after the war, by people in the medical business, that she would never be able to give birth and survive, was lying in her bed again, four years later, with a second girl in her arms. My father and our doctor laughed because they were alive in this balmy night and death had no place in their thoughts, for a few hours at least, and the jenever made them happy enough to brandish their glasses and sing a little.

Like mad *hassidim* they sounded, my mother would tell me. But the story of my birth did not interest me that much. By the time I was able to understand it, I preferred the bits about the laughing and the drinking and the regained happiness of my parents. How they had filled in some gaps in their family. I loved the silver box and beaker with my name on it, they were the presents for my mother because she had given birth. They're in my house now, sometimes with a bit of a black shadow on them because they're badly polished.

And so I started to live with my parents. Early years in which they let their new house to foreigners, and swapped the storms and the cold light, the thorns of the dune roses and the arid marram grass, for the azure coast of France.

Every morning they carried us down the lush mountains to the Mediterranean and every noon the old bus drove us back up. Or so my father told me. I was too small to remember, though I am sure that was when my love for the South crept into my skin.

But I do still remember the sweet scent of the dune roses in Bergen aan Zee, once we had moved back there. As I remember the honeysuckle and all the nature that surrounded me when, aged five, I ran off out of my classroom.

I ran off because the other children had told me I was weird for not celebrating some kind of festivity with my grandparents. I said I had no grandparents, and they called me a liar. I ran away and walked five miles, all the way home. Past houses and then through the woods, where there was nobody alive but me and the trees. My mother and father were outside the house, white with worry after they had received a phonecall from my kindergarten to say I had gone missing. I was so tired then; I slept in clean white sheets all through the afternoon and woke to the living, sweet scent of the dune roses.

Years later I am back for a visit in this village of Bergen aan Zee, with my daughter, playing in the park. Her grandmother is playing with her, turning and turning the little toy horse around, while I stand at the top of some wooden stairs overgrown with dune roses. Their scent reminds me of waking up to the fact that I had to tell the truth about my grandparents: that I had none. Now I take in the sweet smell and with it comes a new kind of feeling, something is whole because my daughter does have a grandmother.

My work is my voice. My voice takes me to sing in places. My music has turned me into a wanderer. And so I go.

RIGA 2006

AT NIGHT THE plane flies over Riga, the capital of Latvia.

I look down on an abundantly-lit city. While we slow down and ease our way toward the runway I see a picture-perfect place. Even from the air, the beautifully conserved architecture of this once so rich and important trading harbour is already visible. I make my way past the new part of town and the Opera House, to the place where I am going to stay. It is the area with the magnificent buildings designed by the architect Eisenstein, father of the famous director of the film *Battleship Potemkin*. Even from behind the car windows I can see we are entering the realm of Jugendstil architecture in all its unspoilt glory. In my gilded and decorated apartment, I rest my hands on the ceramic stove, glance at the ornate ceiling and go to sleep on a sculpted bed. The next morning I wander around with my neck stretched out to admire the houses, gables and streets. I come across the ateliers of Jewish musicians and composers, the houses of the families of famous men of letters and the philosopher Isaiah Berlin. They were honoured with plaques mentioning that these families were 'Russian', or in case of the philosopher Isaiah Berlin, 'British'. Soon it became clear to me that ethnic Latvians had never accepted these Riga-born Jews as Latvians, and did not appreciate the fact that the city of Riga was once dominated by a flourishing Jewish intelligentsia and community of artists. Medical care was developed to the highest standards, discoveries were made and, on the Sabbath, a large part of the Jewish population flocked to the liberal synagogues. They brought visitors with them, often opulent traders from Russia. I imagine they played music and went to concerts in the evenings, or went to see comtemporary plays at the theatre. My grandmother's family visited Riga. Bankers and merchants, they stayed with prominent families and were part of the set of art patrons and enthusiasts. They were from Odessa, where they had built up a fortune. Diamonds and pearls in the Jugendstil style were bought, and presumably worn to dinner parties and such. Until it was stolen, I occasionally wore my grandmother's diamond necklace, a surviving object from another era. When my ancestors decided that Riga was not exciting enough for their lifestye, and no longer slaked their thirst for novelty in the arts, they moved their funds and trades to Paris, and later to the city of Antwerp in Belgium. There, my grandmother was born, still a Russian, but with parents who now spoke French. Wrapped as a baby in lace and fine linen, she remained a Russian till the all too early end of her life.

But I am getting ahead of myself. I want to remain in the nineteenth century atmosphere brimming with developments, and my forefathers walking along these same streets, fully confident in their way of life, yet despised by the ethnic Latvians and Balts who shared their city. How could I be so sure of this undecurrent of negative feeling towards these thriving Jews?

On my way to do some work I came across the 'Jews in Latvia' Museum. I stood for a while, having a hard time remembering street names in Latvian and knowing that today music was on my mind, but that I would come back the next day to see what the museum had to offer. I wrote down the name of the *iela* in a notebook and strolled through the park that my ancestors must have strolled through. Probably with a lot more style than me.

The next day was a drizzly one. I headed for the museum in a neutral mood. The horrors of World War II were part of me, after all. It turned out I was badly prepared for this visit.

The building was large and empty and I made for the top floor, where I found a vaudeville theatre that had once catered to the Yiddish-speaking community. A six-hundred seater with a good stage. I climbed on the stage, started a song to test the acoustics and closed my eyes to hear the laughter and the voices, the orchestra tuning up. I imagined it all in that chilly, empty space. I closed the doors and went down to the first floor where there was a small museum display. An old lady sat, weary, behind a table and made us pay to look at portraits and photographs of people who all looked familiar to me. Like family members, they were. Like some of the few pictures of mine I still had at home. I felt uneasy, and wanted to leave. Then, the old lady asked me if I had seen their extraordinary footage of the German occupation of Riga. It had been shot by a German naval officer on leave. He was invited by his fellow officers to film the round-up and murder of the Jewish people in Riga, and was so shocked by what he saw that he kept the film and handed it over to the Allies after the war.

A film. Black and white, no sound. A bit indifferent, I sit down to watch the document.

I see Latvians and soldiers come out into the streets and pull doctors out of hospital buildings. Shot in the neck, they lie face down in the street, dressed in their suits and bowties. I see elegant, fur-coated women being thrown on a truck, losing their heels, looking as surprised as they are distressed by what is happening to them. I see a small orchestra of neatly arranged young girls, looking very much like my own daughter, being dragged out onto the cobblestones of yet another street and shot. Pleated skirts around their knees, sometimes with a fist clenched round their bows or violins they lie there, eyes open, as if about to get up again. I keep watching in terror as these people are finished off. It happens so fast. At the end of the film it says the Latvians stunned the Gestapo by their zeal: within days of the Germans entering the city, the locals had murdered hundreds of Jews, burning some of them alive in their synagogues.

To then cherish the buildings these people had designed, the knowledge and art they had left behind, as their own Latvian heritage.

Nine burnt-out synagogues are left. The ghetto that 20,000 Jews were brought to, and the inefficiently bulldozed cemetery, remain.

We are well into the twenty-first century, but as I stumble down the cobblestoned Moskova Iela, a straight road to Moscow, I see shacks and cabins behind dishevelled gates. This was the ghetto for the Riga Jews. Doors are hanging open on broken hinges: it looks as if they left a week ago for their final destination. At first I don't notice that I am standing on the remains of a Jewish cemetery. There is little to be found in the way of a monument to acknowledge this tragedy in the history of humanity. Feeling inadequate and miserable, I start humming lines from the Kaddish, the prayer for the dead. Although I never pray, I sing.

Bits of tombstones are sticking out of the razed cemetery, for some reason all these carefully planted trees have grown tall and are completly black. A phenomenon that nobody wants or cares to explain.

Dogs bark at me at the entrance of this sad place and I brave the blank stares of a couple of locals. Out of here is where I should be. I am only too happy to leave.

When I return to my home in Dublin I fall ill. An angry fever rages in my body and I keep dreaming that I lose all my limbs and subsequently feel the pain this loss causes.

That officer filmed them and the onlookers stood there, never thinking of helping. I cannot get rid of the image of the smooth faces of those young girls in their white blouses, their instruments still warm from being used, maybe for a Haydn suite. Extinguished like vermin in the beautiful streets of Riga. My mind seeks for a place of hiding for them and for me. Until I realize that I don't need one. My relatives did, but nobody thought of protecting them.

MOTHER'S PARENTS

IN THE YEAR 2011, I open a book by a well-known American music critic and I come across a small photograph of the world-famous composer: 'Gustav Mahler on the beach in Scheveningen, 1903'.

It looks to me like the same photograph that my grandfather took. When I check with my sister, who still lives in Holland, if it could be the photograph, it turns out there were two copies; one is still in our mother's desk at my sister's home, and the other picture went to the Amsterdam City Archives. In the quiet of a Dublin afternoon I look at the page and the man on the beach in the picture. He is frail but has a certain nonchalance, his hat pushed back and his coat thrown over his shoulders. Unsmiling, but with a pleasant aura of confidence about him. I know this is Gustav Mahler but I am aching to see the man who took that picture: my grandfather.

The first time I saw this picture the wind from the sea was howling around our house, blowing hard into the flames of our stove. My mother was reading a book with the cat in her lap. I was seven years old and I felt safe in my surroundings. I decided to climb onto my mother's chair and seat myself at her desk. It was made of dark mahogany and had sculpted little pillars at the side. It was a treasure of secret drawers I was not allowed to play with. In fact it was my grandmother's desk.

For a while I sat there drawing, my sketchbook open on the green felt, feeling the kind eyes of my grandmother on me. A small portrait of her in a silver frame stands right above me on the desk. Her curly hair in a bun on top of her head, a high-necked lace blouse. She is holding a baby: my eldest uncle, the one who was shot on the beach. I had heard my mother talk about him. That was not what I wanted to think about, so I slipped off the chair and dug into the dressing-up chest in the corridor. Once I had pinned up my hair, I donned a long velvety gown and drowned my little arms in endless gloves. In front of the mirror, I thought I had achieved a likeness of my grandmother's style and went back to sit behind the desk to take up my drawing again. Not for long though. Two pictures had fallen out of one of the secret drawers. One was a small photo of a man in a hat and coat standing on a beach. I wondered who it was: 'Mummy?'. My mother looked up from her book, inhaled deeply from her cigarette and stared at me. I had disturbed her with my question, and now I wanted to stir up memories. 'Oh child,' she said, 'that is a picture of the Austrian composer Gustav Mahler. Your grandfather took it when he was out for a walk with him and Mr R. on the beach in Scheveningen.'

It meant nothing to me. We wore pleated dresses and patent leather shoes when we went to hear the Bach Passions performed by the Concertgebouw Orchestra, or watch Mozart's operas at the theatre. I played little baroque pieces on my wooden flute, but at the age of seven, Mahler's outstandingly beautiful symphonies and songs were a music I had not yet been introduced to. The only thing that sparked my attention was my mother mentioning Mr R. from Wassenaar. I knew him as the man with the large house and larger park on the outskirts of The Hague. He had goats and sheep grazing on his land and, when my mother's entire family came to stay over, the children were allowed to go for a drive in what my mother called the goat-cart. I always imagined six curly heads screaming and shouting in a small wooden cart pulled by giant goats racing around the estate, while the adults wandered down from the big house through the park to have tea in a folly that R. had built.

That big house and the land were confiscated by the Gestapo in 1940, who then used it as their headquarters for that area. Before it was torn down in 1947, many people were tortured and killed in that stunning building where Mr R. and my grandfather plotted how to

finance the performances of Gustav Mahler's work and how to bring
the great composer over from Vienna to Holland while their wild
offspring raced around the gardens.

My grandfather dealt in ships and travelled the world, but his
great interests in life were music and sports. Together with Mr R. the
famous music patron, he invested money in trying to bring the Dutch
public up to scratch with contemporary classical music.

In 1903 and 1904 Gustav Mahler travelled to the Netherlands to
introduce his work. It was played by the Concertgebouw Orchestra
and conducted by Mengelberg, a fanatical admirer of Mahler's work
who later would became a notorious collaborator with the Nazi
regime. In 1940 he denounced Mahler's music as Jewish music, and
therefore inaudible and unplayable.

> *Years later when I was studying music in The Hague at the
> Royal Conservatoire, we often drove past that lonely folly in
> Wassenaar, the only building left of Mr R.'s estate, and my
> mother never failed to point it out to me. Some things had
> stayed put.*

I see my grandfather walking on the beach with his friend Mr R.
and the great composer Gustav Mahler discussing developments in the
music world in Europe. How difficult it had been for the village boy
Mahler, the *Jew* Mahler, to enter the Viennese musical arena. How
happy he was that his work was going to be celebrated and recognized
in Holland. Recognition, that's what I saw in Mahler's attitude on the
empty beach. And I see the man beside him, my grandfather. Short,
lively, gesticulating, as if to emphasize his admiration, absorbing
the treasures that the maestro hands out while the large white beach
unrolls itself before them. They are walking close to the lapping waves
in early autumn, a dull day, warm enough to take off their coats. The
sea is just another presence in this picture.

I know they had lunch at the Kurhaus Grand Hotel in Scheveningen,
the names of composers resonating around my grandfather's ears like

incisive musical notes: Schoenberg, Berg, Zemlinksky, Webern. He was eager to learn about vocal scores, his first love in music. The Kurhaus restaurant must have been buzzing with minor royalty, wealthy guests and stars of that time. Nobody paid any attention to these three loud men who were were enjoying their fish and their lively conversation.

So many decades later, when the Kurhaus has declined and been converted to a concert hall, I am to sing there for the first time, Bach's St Matthew Passion. *Ignorant of the fact that my grandfather was here as a music lover in the presence of the great Mahler. Ignorant, back then, of so many facts about my family. Just a happy teenager strolling on the beach with a boy after the concert.*

After their lunch the gentlemen are driven back to Wassenaar. Later that evening, at the house of Mr R. where they are spending the night, grandfather dares to sing a few songs for maestro Mahler. They all wonder why he does not sing professionally, even the conductor Mengelberg, who has joined them and accompanies my grandfather at the grand piano. My grandfather, suddenly withdrawn and shy, explains that he comes from a very strict family background where singing in public or, even worse, on a stage for money, is considered a low-life occupation.

The conductor Mengelberg is so grateful to be with maestro Mahler, and to be collecting the subsidies for his orchestra. He relishes the company of these men in evening dress, the lavish food and the comfort of deeply intelligent conversation. Men who, some years on, he will not fail to reduce to a 'filthy race' and despise for their very existence.

That day on the beach was theirs, and they triumphed in their musical endeavours. I feel proud of my grandfather.

Remembering now, as a seven-year-old back at home in my native village with the storm raging, sitting by the stove in my blue velvet gown and elbow gloves, being brought back even further, to one of my grandparents' houses on that same seashore my home was built on. Listening to my mother talk about her youth. She said they, her parents, used go to Amsterdam to attend concerts and plays all the time. They had the house in Amsterdam of course, where she was born, but they preferred the sea air and they had bigger stables in Zandvoort. She explains: stables for the horses, when they travelled by carriage, before her time. When the motor car arrived it was even easier to drive to the city and back.

I listened to my mother's stories of that familiar wind tearing around their house, just like it blew around my ears in our home. My mother would have snuggled up in bed waiting for my grandmother to come up to kiss her goodnight.

Sometimes, mother continued, my mother would button up her shoes sitting on my bed. Her blue taffeta underskirts all around her, a long hook in her hand to handle her boots. A cloud of Mitsouko perfume holding her together. Singing a bit of the music they were about to hear, softly, so I would drift away. But I was too happy, watching my mother's profile against the flicker of the fire, her hair up, her diamond earrings and necklace sparkling on and off as she moved her head.

The nervous shuffle of the horses in front of their carriage underneath the windows had been replaced by the more monotonous deep roar of their car waiting to take them away. My mother was left with the rustling sounds of silks, hasty steps down the stairs, laughing, and a whiff of perfume to keep her company in her sleep.

My grandparents had their seats at the concert hall in Amsterdam and people were looking forward to admiring my grandmother's latest outfits. My mother delighted in describing the evening gowns her mother wore, as if they were nearly separate beings that gracefully accepted my grandmother inhabiting their exquisite form and fabric. Hand-painted and embroidered silks that my grandfather brought over from his trips to China were fitted on her by Parisian couturiers, in order to dazzle.

Dazzle who? I wondered, while I rearranged the folds of my own gown and fumbled at my hairdo, feeling that a bit of my grandmother's glamour had come to me.

My wonderful glamorous grandmother who, with the exotic feathers in her hat trembling with conviction, did not shy from standing up for women's rights in the most high-toned establishments in Amsterdam and The Hague, or in London, a city she often visited. If she had the feeling that her words were going unheard, she would jump up on a café table and start waving her umbrella or parasol around so as to attract maximum attention. Her impressive outfits and good looks seemed to have helped that cause rather than obstruct it.

Once, when she was on a London trip, after a passionate tirade at the Dorchester in favour of independent women, she was approached by the grandson of Thomas Cook, who befriended her and my grandfather. He asked my grandmother to be his guinea pig and explore Venice as a single woman on a Cook's tour. After consulting her husband she agreed to travel on her own to Italy. She left Holland with numerous suitcases, stayed six weeks in the Lido Hotel in Venice and came home with twenty suitcases filled with clothes and fabrics. Porcelain, glass and paintings followed in wooden cases. And a set of rare eighteenth century French silver.

My mother brandished a silver spoon at me in the middle of her story, all that was left of that French silver set. She would tell me the spoon story later.

So she goes on about her home and the six children embracing their glamorous mother, back from Italy, while their nurse is trying to hold them back from opening all the cases and trying on the Italian clothes and shoes, secretly swooning herself over the silk of the stockings between her fingers. There are presents for everybody and food to be cooked that the kitchen maids handle with disdainful care.

When my grandfather arrives to welcome his wife back into their home, she immediately suggests that they should organize a party. He shakes his head no, but then agrees when she waves piles of scores by Italian composers in front of him. She has bought them for him to sing.

My cheeks were burning and, with the light going out of the day, my mother's tales became more mysterious, as if they were detaching themselves from our family history.

That winter, she said, there were some exotic animals from Circus Elleboog, monkeys, giraffes and camels, spending the winter in the stables of our seaside town. We, the children, had been asked if we would like to ride the female camel sometime.

While the polishing and cooking for the party is underway they go, the children and their mother, to the beach. My grandmother's frizzy hair blows in her face and her hat dances away in the wind. The children race the camel along the beach. My mother holds her mother's hand and repeats after her – Tintoretto, Titian – names of wonderful picture painters from Venice while they walk on the white sand. A bunch of children run past them and scream 'dirty Jewess' at my grandmother. She laughs and ignores them.

My mother follows the flock of ugly little stingers, as she calls them later, with her eyes. A couple walks by and greets them, remarking that these children seem to be born to ride camels. It must be in their blood, they say. They were the big stingers, my mother said. Time to go home for our party, her mother told her, looking forward to music and food and dances and dresses. She squeezed her tiny child's gloved hand tightly.

That takes me to the birth of another little girl on the Prinsengracht in Amsterdam, on 22 June 1988, with the Dutch population raving on the canals, their faces dipped in orange paint to emphasize their nationalistic pride in their football team's victory in the European Championship. Underneath my hospital window I can hear howls and shouts while my daughter is being born to another team of orange faces and fake plastic noses; doctors and nurses in disguise, who have fallen for Dutch pride. We laugh a lot. To me it all seems a strange circus and I wonder why I have my little S. under such surreal circumstances. Go Holland. GO!

A few hours later I am at home and I hear my parents' car, its loud motor rumbling and rattling over the cobblestones of the canal where we live.

They burst into the bedroom and I watch their bushy silver heads bend over the baby. A new grandchild we called Saar. My father, fragile in his old frame, starts to shake and flees down the stairs to our living room. My mother goes to check on him. Ten minutes later she comes back to tell me that my father was crying because my daughter is called after his beloved sister, the only Saar he has loved. Up till now I say, but then even the chiming of my little one's new toy suddenly sounds sad to me. To cheer me up, my mother hands me a present wrapped in a piece of cloth. The silver survivor spoon, she jokes.

In the end, she did tell me the story of that French silver spoon. On 22 June 1940 in Zandvoort, my mother and her eldest brother are alone in the house on the sea shore. The air is hazy with heat and, although they are having a sombre discussion about their situation, they decide to forget their worries for an hour and go for a swim. A run down the dunes, a dive in the chilly North Sea waves, seems like the best of futures for now. They go to change and my mother is the first one back down in the hall in her striped suit and a loose jacket, a towel wrapped around her slim hips. There is a bang on the front door. There are no more staff left, so she opens the heavy front door herself. A bunch of German soldiers push her aside and head straight upstairs. A moment later a high-ranking officer arrives, looks around the hall and tells my mother: 'This is an excellent house, we will take it'. More soldiers come in and order her to go pack some belongings. Ten minutes. She packs fast, two suitcases for herself and for her brother who must have heard something and has escaped via the backstairs and door. She rushes down to the pantry.

The backdoor is open, he is gone. Already all the cupboards have been opened and emptied by the soldiers; a dresser stands blind and hollow with its drawers pulled out. In their thieving frenzy they dropped one spoon on the floor, part of the eighteenth century French set brought back from Venice. She picks it up and puts it in the pocket of her jacket. She knows she could get shot for this. After all, this spoon is now the property of the German Reich. A moment later she drags two suitcases down the stairs and through the front door. That's what they have allowed her to keep. And the bathing suit she is still wearing.

The spoon has its place in my birth beaker. It lives where we live and even if it always stays empty, because we don't use it for its normal purpose, it still feeds us memories.

There was that other photograph that had fallen out of my grandmother's desk. The words 'nobody sleeps' are written on the back.

It is a picture of my grandfather, in gala evening attire, standing at the head of a table of about a hundred imposing-looking people. Clearly, he is singing. 'Yes,' my mother said, 'he was.' Singing in that clear, strong tenor voice of his.

In the late thirties, her parents had moved back to their house in Amsterdam because the winters had become too harsh in Zandvoort. They were both in their mid-fifties and for some anniversary my grandmother suggested a trip to the Lido in Venice where she had spent such wonderful days. My grandfather agreed to combine a business meeting with the pleasure of returning to Venice.

They traveled by train to Italy, my grandmother clutching her favourite book, *The Man Without Qualities* by Robert Musil, my grandfather with his papers and scores in the leather satchel he always insisted on carrying himself. The servants travelled with their luggage in a different section of the train.

When they arrived at the Lido by vaporetto, they immediately went to the beach, took their shoes off, dipped their toes in the lukewarm water and had tea served. They were seated in those same deckchairs where the composers Mahler and Stravinsky had sat looking out into the past of Venice, savouring the richness of the present, dreaming while the beautiful young bodies walked by.

That night my grandfather sang. He sang Puccini, with an open throat and an excellent technique, with an abandon that almost made his business colleagues uneasy. It was the last time he sang in public. A few years later my mother was alone with only that picture and some others, having lost the people in them to a war.

It is a Dublin evening now. The wind has died down, some silent darkness is pressing against the window. I see the reflection of myself, unclear. With the lamp behind me I can pretend it is me as a child. I can remember home. How I had opened my mouth, imitating the man in the photograph, thinking I could hear him, my grandfather, sing. How I wanted to sing like him. Sing in that clean, silver timbre, free in its precision. He was in control of his music in his short life when he sang that aria: '*Nessun dorma*', nobody sleeps.

MOTHER

OUR ULTIMATE conversation lasted some three months.

My mother was living in Bergen again, the place where I was born in North Holland. I was still living in Amsterdam, with my Irish husband and our little daughter.

Her room is filled with flowers and books. 'Finally, we have some time to talk about the past,' she says. I stroke the liver spots on her hand, thinking that it is final indeed.

Mother will die soon. She is lying on her deathbed, suffering from terminal cancer. There is no pain, a tube bites her hand and I can see the drops of morphine falling from the bag: a slow countdown. She has a few months left to live, to tell me about all these days in her past.

I have been reading to her, from her favoured authors, the poet Paul Celan in particular, and also a lot of short stories in different languages. She still hasn't lost her eagerness to demonstrate how well she knows her languages. And how much literature she has devoured in her life. In her opinion there is always another language and a new author to discover. She used to teach us sentences in Norwegian during dinner. They have stayed in my head, words belonging to mother's world.

She smiles when she starts talking about her past, first the pleasant things that I do know something about, she promises, but with more details.

While I brush the silver back into her curls she looks at my hand and the antique diamond ring on my finger, a so-called rosette diamond from Amsterdam, a customary part of the dowry of the Sephardic

Jews who originated from Spain. Always the grande dame, she acknowledges the sentimental worth of this pretty piece of jewellery. But it is not a Bolshevik, the last of the diamond rings that she owned; those she had swapped for food in 1944 while hiding from the Nazis in a friend's house.

They bought her meat with that diamond ring, meat that she could not eat or digest. She shrugs in her high hospital bed at the thought of it. She could no more eat then than she can now.

I am getting used to her drifting into a short daydream like that, or clinging onto a shred of memory. We are in my father's old workroom where she has said she wants to die, among his books, and she sits up in her simple nightgown ready to tell me about a dress that she had had made for herself, for a party at age … eighteen. It was not that she was going to tell me all about every party she went to, she says, and laughs at the idea.

I wonder how many parties there might have been.

It was just about that one party. She went to see Miss Honing who made the evening dresses for her and her sisters, and sometimes for her mother. She had made her a black dress with a décolletage and a bow at the small of her back. She wore a *petit gris* fur because it wasn't that warm the night they went out to dance.

All day she had been learning by heart some poem by the Russian poet Pushkin, whom she had recently discovered, and she annoyed the young man who brought her to the dance by reciting it all out loud in Russian. He told her in his polite manner that he had trouble understanding her. Surely meaning, in fact, that she was an attractive snob, she says to me, as if she is still eighteen and flirtatious. She laughs again. She says she forgot all about it when the trumpet player came out with the orchestra in the ballroom of the hotel. He was called Louis Armstrong. He blew life into their feet to make them dance, until she fell flat on the dance floor at around midnight.

She had lost her bow, it fell off her dress while dancing, and she stuffed it in her evening bag on her way to the deli. The only one open so late at night. They, her friends and her, were all set for a few sandwiches made by Hijman Mok. Hijman was witty and sharp and he made the best sandwiches in the world. His shop was narrow and clean and he served gherkins, pickled lemons, onions, you name it.

That night Hijman had a young man behind the counter with him. He looked very intellectual with his glasses and short moustache, and he made no attempt to serve them. She asked him what he was doing working for Hijman. He said he was his son and no good at the sandwich business at all. My mother wondered what he was good at then, poetry maybe? She joked a little about it and, as she opened her purse to pay for the food, she didn't notice the bow from her dress fall on the shop floor.

They were already on their way home when the young man caught up with them and handed her the bow. She thought he was rather strange and asked her friends did they know anything about him. Oh yes, that is Maurits Mok the poet, he has already published some important work, they told her. His father is very proud of his children, the sister plays the piano. My mother was a bit taken aback by her own remarks, and hoped she had not been too condescending. She was only eighteen and her sophisticated world was very small then.

Maurits had been watching her, and did not forget that young beauty in her fur, nor the bow she dropped that night.

She, however, and she smiles a little when she tells me this, forgot all about him until they met again in 1947.

She had been invited to a poetry reading in the main café in the town of Laren, which was an artists' colony with many prominent writers, composers and painters living there at the time. The well-known poet Mok was reading in the restaurant and a crowd had gathered. Mok had lost his entire family, some of her friends who were there told her. She was alone as well.

After his reading he came up to her and said straight away to her that he recognized her, that they knew each other from the sandwich shop. Mother wondered what a poet was doing in that shop? Picking up the bow that she had torn off her outrageous ball gown, he joked.

Then she remembered. All gone, those ball gowns and the furs, all those times, she said, while she coughed loudly.

She remembered his father Hijman, the small man who was so funny and clever and she inquired about him. Maurits did not answer. All hers were mostly gone as well she said, and coughed again.

Her illness, that she had contracted during the war, was playing up. Back then, before the war, Maurits did not dare come near her, but now here they were, with their shared passion for literature, and their dead. It was the dead who brought them together in the small town of Laren.

That night they outdid each other, quoting poems loudly, she in flawless English, he with an understanding of verse that she had not come across before. All her beloved icons came to life and spent the rest of the evening being tossed about in the summer air. She was fascinated by this strange man.

A week later he went to find her and proposed. She was resting, having been diagnosed with another bout of tuberculosis. She was sitting fully dressed on the bed, her legs covered by a tartan rug, reading a book of poems by Maurits Mok. When he asked her to marry him, she hesitated because one of the first things he had told her was that his sandwich-making skills were non-existent. As were hers. She had not mastered the art of cooking during her life with her parents, and during the years of war there was nothing to cook with.

For three arduous months he came to see her, read to her and made her laugh. The war was not mentioned between them.

It was a warm summer in 1948 and he would cycle home in the dark after these long visits. Home was an acquaintance's garage which had been transformed into a living space with a sink and a small bathroom. It had a bed, a sofa, a table and a lot of shelves where he put his books and papers. His artist friends had given him some paintings. He had two large photographs on the wall. One was of his sister Saar and him as little children. Saar, with her dark eyes and her serious bow in her hair, and Mozes, as he was called then, blonde and blue-eyed. Neither of them were smiling. The second picture was of his parents all dressed up to go to a wedding, walking down a road.

The garage was built separately from the house, which belonged to an eccentric professor of literature and stood in the middle of a small wood. It was quiet and he felt there was enough breathing space for him to regain a sense of freedom. To listen to his ramshackle radio. The crackling sounds of his beloved Chopin études.

He wanted to be able to reshape the silence; the one containing all those murdered voices that he needed to describe in his work. Mother and I are both thinking of one of his earliest poems after the war ...

... He wore a green suit, mother's voice fills me in again, made from an apple-green fabric, the only one he was able to buy with his textile coupons. Thin as a fish bone with the suit flapping about him, his thick hair half-covered by a dark hat, a badly trimmed moustache and a torn leather bag full of books under his arm, he could have stepped straight out of a Charlie Chaplin film as the Tramp.

He brought writers with him when he visited her, among them a man who told her he was a cardinal in the church of W.B. Yeats and had travelled to Ireland to meet the great poet. They talked and laughed at her bedside, and hoped that she would marry their friend.

When she was allowed to get out of bed for a couple of hours a day they went out to meet a great friend of my father, a well-known poet. They had a cup of tea and, while Maurits read some of his friend's new work, she and the friend went out for a walk, past the neighbour's neatly trimmed hedges and gardens dense with roses and jasmine. Through the fields where they picked some wild flowers. At dusk they went back past the gardens and jumped over the hedges to steal the roses. It was only two years since the war was over and nobody could afford flowers.

She is tired and looks at the lavish bunches of flowers in her room. Could I give her some sugar water she asks. Her eyes close when I dab her mouth with something sweet. She takes my hand and whispers that she likes sugar. Her sister's child needed sugar, her sister had stolen sugar in the *Jappenkamp*, and they hung her by her wrists in the sun. I go to the window and slowly, softly, close the curtains on the evening, on this other story that is too much for now, too much for me.

When she sleeps, I sleep.

We have breakfast together. She watches me eat and drink. The nurse checks her drip while I talk to my family on the phone.

Mother asks if she can tell me more, she feels up to it this morning, she thinks. I let her talk ...

'My father said I could do anything I liked, but he was opposed to the idea of me going on the stage to act. I never understood that. He did so much for artists and had the deepest respect for them. He spent all his time with them. He sang at home and made me perform in front of his friends.' Suddenly she drifts into a slumber but when she wakes up she mumbles 'A strange Calvinistic streak he had.' Her father, my grandfather ... never losing track of her story, my story ...

I am in the living room practising a piece by a Dutch composer. She likes to hear me sing, and she knew him and his brothers, all composers, when they were boys. Their uncle, the sculptor, made a bust of her. He spied on her from his atelier windows when she skipped school. His atelier was in the alleyway that she used to escape from school. He opened a window and called down to her, asked her if she wanted to come up and sit for him. She did. Which one of her schoolmistresses was ever going to find her in there? A safe skip.

Yes, I tell her how I remember that sculptor in deep conversation with my parents on our terrace in Bergen aan Zee. I liked the look of this man, he was famous for his statues of the designer of the Afsluitdijk, the longest dyke in Holland, the engineer Cornelis Lely. His statue stood tall in between two seas, looking out over the end of the land of Holland.

And then *De Dokwerker* statue, a dockworker, in honour of the strike these workmen held during the war to protest against the deportation of Jews. This statue was in Amsterdam: it stood broad in front of the Portuguese Synagogue, the *Esnoga*, glaring in defiance, while pigeons searched for food between the cobblestones at his feet. I had seen both statues.

This man, with his long white mane, drinking beer, cursing those fat curses that sounded good to me. I tried them out on my class mates. They seemed horrified.

He, my mother says, was a friend who came to our parties at your grandparents where I recited long poems … I listen to her recite with difficulty, the words stuck between her dry lips.

In 1931 it was decided by her family that she would move to England for a few years. She looks at the trees in the garden while I sponge her back and lift her up to change her bed.

'Hats,' she says. 'I went to see Madame Cluzet in Amsterdam for hats before sailing to England. She was the best hat maker in Holland and she complained about my unruly curls. I wore my hair short and flattened it with hair creams but it wouldn't stay flat. I bought the creams because I liked the design on the boxes as much as I liked the hat boxes.

'I loved Madame Cluzet, her real name was Cohen. She was French and very insistent in her ideas of how women should move about in the world: elegantly hatted and with their own jobs and money. She was a stubborn woman, who ended up as an experiment for Dr Mengele. He probably made something out of her skin once he had ripped out her womb.'

A dead bitter silence follows. She turns her back to me and whispers that she would like some water.

And then she continues: 'So, I did not want to go to England, but I was young and obedient and I went. With my hats. I would have liked to have seen more of my family during that whole period and to have talked with my brothers and sisters. We only had a few years together and then I continued talking to them in my thoughts. For the rest of my life.'

She likes her clean bed and when I lower her on it as if she is my child, so small and thin, she sighs. 'That's nice Judith, no pain at all, much better than at the end of the war, when I was lying in the dark with a stomach full of broken glass, that's what it felt like, and I heard their barking outside in the street, German soldiers. I could not turn my body around and then there was the drone of the planes, British and American bombers. The hope that they would save me numbed my fear and the pain. I never cried. I'd heard that my brother had been shot by the Japanese. He was the one I needed most. It was dark and cold during the days and the nights. My only activity was chewing on pieces of paper, rather than on tulip bulbs, which were apparently healthy food. I still love tulips though,' she says. We laugh.

England, 1931. They sent her there to distract her from the things she really wanted to do, like acting and singing. They wanted her to forget about her own life and passions and live the life of another girl. The one who picked up her very posh accent in English. Who spent time in Bristol and Brighton, where she wore green silk trousers and stayed at hotels that had a winter garden. Trying not to get too bored, swapping one dashing gown for the next and one dashing fiancé for the other. Curtsied for the King and then went back to put on those green trousers that were the talk of the town. Going around England with her friends, having picnics in fields full of flowers. With their chauffeur sitting at a safe distance, eating his sandwiches. She liked the chauffeur; he taught her how to drive. She liked the Bentley. She did not like the empty conversations, the babble, with her friends.

In fact, all she liked was her books and the plays her hosts took her to see. She read about real life in the books of the poets and the novelists of modern England and sneaked out to meet them. And she started singing. Singing? I was just about to tell her to have a rest, she is suddenly talking so much, but now I need to hear more, selfishly.

Yes, at the hotel in Brighton there were American musicians composing songs at the piano in their rooms. She used to walk past the open windows on the ground floor and, she pauses for a moment of suspense; they played her favourite song whenever she walked by. They invited her in and asked her if she could sing. She sang along with them, in that dark, raw voice of hers. They encouraged her and complimented her on her trousers.

Did she only have the one pair I venture to ask? 'Oh, it was revolutionary to wear them,' she says, indignant, 'I got myself an orange pair as well.'

Four years of England, and an Englishness that she adopted with grace.

She integrated, as we all learnt to integrate, to mould ourselves to the society we lived in, so we would go unnoticed as Jews.

First she taught my father how to pronounce his English correctly, then she taught us, the children. This obsessive need to possess a language and be able to express yourself fluently in it had turned into some kind of virtue for her. You had to be perfect at it or else there was the risk that you could betray yourself. A fear ingrained in our subconscious? To be different during these times meant expulsion, death.

1935 and she is back in Holland, matured, and determined to push through to a stage career. She contacts her parent's influential friends and auditions for well-known directors. Her mentor and support is an influential architect. He gives her a first edition of Oscar Wilde's *Salomé* and dedicates it with the obvious 'Off with his head!', referring to John the Baptist in the play and the original biblical story, and all those who are unwilling to take her on as an actress.

> *When I sing my first major part in an opera she gives me that book, with her own dedication: 'To my darling Judith, keep your head on!'*

There are rumors of tragedy from relatives and friends who come to stay with them. Rumours about Germany and the Jews. Her brothers climb mountains, row in national championships, or play tennis on the court at the back of the house. These last seasons before the war go by in comfort, and the serious discussions about fascism are always wrapped in wonderful meals and luxurious surroundings.

Although she is passionate about her acting there is that tendency in her for learning and reading and travelling with a coterie of friends. A trip to France lasts six months and she finds herself mixing with a crowd of artists. She's eager to perfect her French and deepen her insight into contemporary painting. 'I was slow at life and learning,' she sighs. 'So slow.'

At the age of twenty-six she finds herself pregnant and, against her parents' wishes (they want her to marry Baron S.), she goes to Switzerland and has an abortion. 'And a good thing it was that I did not bring an unwanted child into a world that was going to be destroyed.' She sounds proud of her independence and insights, even now. And I am proud of her too.

And then comes the time in 1940 when she buys a passage on the boat to America, to New York. She will stay with friends to start with, and of course audition for the great theatres. Two of her brothers and one sister are in the Dutch East Indies, the colony of Indonesia, the other sister is in France married to a Bulgarian doctor and her eldest brother lives in Holland, like her.

A week before she is about to sail, staying with her brother who lives close to the port of Rotterdam, she becomes very ill with the flu. The doctor advises her to stay in bed, she is not well enough to travel. It is decided that she will take the next boat.

So she gives her ticket to a girlfriend who badly needs to leave the country as well. That boat was the last one to sail to the USA. Two days later the Germans invaded Holland.

All was lost. She kept some books with her in that suitcase they allowed her to pack before the Germans confiscated the house in Zandvoort. The other houses were confiscated as well. She had nowhere to go and no contact with her family. She knew some people who told her she could stay with them.

She pauses for water.

Should we stop all this talking? I ask. But her emaciated body is burning with an almost ethereal energy, she needs to tell her tale.

I open a window, as if to let out some of this oppressive history and let in some air. It is a late Indian summer. Birds ruffle about, there is a scent of cut grass coming up to us. The nurse comes in and chats with us for the sake of a chat. Life is normal out there.

That is what I say to her, once the nurse has left. 'Oh yes, life is always normal out there,' she sighs. She sighs a lot, my dear mother.

She stayed with friends of the conductor Mengelberg for a while. Soon enough they grew sympathetic to his ideas, and Hitler's ideals. She managed to escape through a window during the night, after she heard them talk about joining the Dutch Nazi party. It was just her luck that she ended up with that lot. 'Bloody creeps. They did prison time after the war. Anyway, I still had my suitcase then. With poems and plays in it. Plays that I was going to be performing in. Soon.'

I see pearls of sweat on her smooth forehead and tell her to wait a while.

I was so proud of her, on that much colder morning, when I closed the book I had been reading to her and she started telling me how sorry she had felt for these children. The German children, victims of war, wandering along the train tracks in Cologne in July 1945. They were putting their little paws on the windows of her compartment. She was lying on a bed in the Red Cross train that was taking her to Davos in Switzerland, to a sanatorium where she might recover from severe tuberculosis. With all lost to her, and living in a body that was burning her up, she still wanted to see what was going on outside in the world, behind the windows of her train. They moved very slowly through the ruins. She saw small children in rags, too tired to even beg. Empty suffering in their eyes. And she thought how their suffering was wrong, just as much as hers. She said her pain was small, because there was not much left to feel. But she must have been aware of these miserable creatures, enough to remember them years later.

The Swiss nurse who accompanied her on the train could not understand why she wanted to give those rag dolls her food, the food that she could not digest anyway. These are German, *Deutsche Kinder*, she shouted at my mother. And my mother answered that it wasn't their fault that they were what they were, and she too had suffered just for being what she was.

So the train drove her to these spectacular mountains where they fed her an endless supply of fatty foods.

Wedding photo of Judith Mok's maternal grandparents, Pieter Timmermans and Cornelia Fransen, Amsterdam 1895.

Gustav Mahler on the beach in Scheveningen, 1906.

Judith Mok's mother, Riemke, with her mother, Cornelia Timmermans-Fransen, in 1915.

Riemke Timmermans-Mok as Mozart in 1927.

Maurits Mok (extreme right) with Joseph Roth (extreme left), Amsterdam 1937.

Judith Mok's paternal grandparents, Hijman Mok and Elisabet Blitz, Haarlem 1938.

```
                  ster 9-1-90 (
  Nathan Streep 18-6-90         ) 4-6-43 S.

  Elisabeth Judith Coster 2-6-01 - 11-6-43 S.
  Elisabeth Mok 9-2-04 - 30-9-42 O.
  Rosette Mok-Katoen 20-5-72 (
  Izaäk Mok 18-9-72           )11-6-43 S.
  Alexander de Vries 12-1-12 - 23-7-43 S.
  Harry de Vries 18-6-13 - 4-6-43 S.

  Simon Verduin 10-8-08 - 4-6-43 S.


  Anna de Solla-Blaaser 17-8-05(
  René de Solla 1-2-30         )11-6-43 S.

  Johanna Aussen-Mok 26-6-03(          (
  Maurits Bernard Henri Aussen 19-5-02)2-7-43 S.

  Salomon Samson 7-1-93 - 2-7-43 S.
  Rebecca Samson-......(....-..-..)
```

Part of a typed document provided by the Red Cross in 1946, listing some of Judith Mok's murdered family members.

Judith Mok's parents, Maurits Mok and Riemke Timmermans, on their wedding day 1948, Laren.

Judith Mok with her father, Maurits Mok, 1960s.

Judith Mok
with Elisabeth
Schwarzkopf,
Amsterdam 198.

Judith Mok with her daughter, Saar O'Loughlin, Amsterdam 1989.

Judith Mok with King Willem-Alexander of the Netherlands and Queen Máxima at the Concertgebouw in Amsterdam after performing at the gala concert for their wedding, 2001.

Zwaantje Mok
1.2.1920 - 24 jaar

Jantje Mok-Benninga
31.10.1873 - 69 jaar

Elisabeth Mok-Blitz
18.4.1879 - 64 jaar

Maria Mok-Blitz
22.1.1873 - 69 jaar

Elisabeth Mok-Blok
4.7.1879 - 63 jaar

Sara Mok-Boers
18.8.1904 - 38 jaar

Bloeme Mok-Boerske
20.9.1870 - 71 jaar

Hadasse Mok
25.4.1931 - 11 jaar

Hartog Mok
11.5.1876 - 66 jaar

Henny Mok
21.10.1919 - 23 jaar

Hermina Mok
1.8.1918 - 24 jaar

Hijman Mok
12.5.1879 - 64 jaar

Hijman Mok
21.6.1916 - 26 jaar

Hugo Mok
21.11.1934 - 9 jaar

The Dutch Holocaust Memorial of Names in Amsterdam with the names of Judith's grandmother Elisabeth Mok-Blitz and grandfather Hijman Mok clearly visible. Courtesy of Marc van Meurs.

'We were naughty you know, we were like teenagers, all these wounded resistance fighters and these miserable survivors, we escaped from our rooms and we smoked ... and sang songs. We were giddy with freedom and food.'

She holds my hand and hums the song that I am familiar with. A Russian song.

'I learned all these songs from Boris in the dark. Sometime in 1944 when we were wandering from hiding place to hiding place and kept meeting the same anxious faces, I met Boris. And his cat. These days you would say that Boris was camp and all that, but that never occurred to me when he was teaching me these songs and calling me *moya radost*, my joy, in Russian.

'We had no light or heating, we had no life, but we had our music. Boris came from Odessa and he became a famous singing teacher. How ironic that I had to meet a great teacher when, for me, there were no stages left to climb on.

'Will you sing for me?' How abruptly she interrupts her story to put me on the spot. She demands Rachmaninov. So I sing while she closes her eyes and very softly calls me *moya radost*, my joy.

I close my eyes to slip away with her and her dreams.

Once a month, mother used to drive us to The Hague. Through the tulip fields, sometimes stubbly and sandy, sometimes like giant unicoloured flags spread out over the horizon. She chatted to me and pointed at the stately houses along the road where her friends had lived, or still did, their lives unchanged by the war. Still loyal friends, she told me.

I know them, these rather strict people who live in warm, large houses and eat scarcely filled sandwiches for lunch. These men and women, with only a hint of a smile around their mouths, never fail to give me a useful present when we go to stay with them at the holidays. A present all the same, carefully wrapped in recycled wrapping paper that lowers my natural excitement about gifts to a degree of polite

*anticipation. With them I try hard to behave as if I belong.
I think these careful people must be exemplary adults and
at the same time I feel, although I am only a child, that I
have already started to fail at this exemplary state and am
developing a fake one on the occasion of obligatory visits
to their world. And yet I know, and this is what gives me a
heavy feeling of dutifulness, that some of these serious friends
of my mother's kept their cold heads clear during a period
when my mother needed to be invisible to the Germans, and
did all they could to help her survive. Which she did. While
we drive past the house of such and such, at a very moderate
speed in our decrepit car, I sigh a long sigh. The weight of
gratitude for my mother's existence and mine is quickly lifted
by the time we drive on to the Lange Voorhout, the beautiful
old square in The Hague where the former Queen of the
Netherlands, Wilhelmina, owned a small palace. Beside her
palace, she had acquired a house for Russian refugees, the one
we were going to visit. I can let go of all restraint in this house
full of highly strung creatures who will never find a peaceful
way to cohabit. Princesses and housemaids, camp survivors
and wood merchants, opera singers and circus artists are all
stacked away in this refuge for lost Russian souls. While my
mother heads for her friend Boris, the famous old singer, I am
pulled into one room after the next. The competition between
them is fierce: who gives the best treats and who tells the best
stories to little curly headed Judith. I pile cookies, sweets and
piroshki, bread stuffed with cabbage, in my stomach and rest
my short legs on embroidered pillows while listening to their
stories. The samovar rattles and the maid is ordered around
by the princess, although technically they now have the same
status. I listen to their stories, told over and over again. It's as
if a giant book has come alive. Dressed in their dated clothes
that look like costumes, they walk up and down in front of
me, their sole audience, and let me decide which pages to turn.*

*With some I travel down the rivers, jumping from log to log,
with others I drink tea with the Tsaritsa and discuss the* beau
monde *of Saint Petersburg, or I attempt to do some tricks with
the circus artist. They insist on making me kiss gold-encrusted
icons of Madonnas. That's the part I dislike and which makes
me decide to join my mother and her friend Boris.*

*Boris is an old man who taught my mother to sing during
the last years of the war. Boris is a quiet man. After fleeing
Russia he had became an important singer and teacher in
Amsterdam until, being of Jewish descent, he was pushed
out of his job by some obliging and cooperative musical
colleagues who were eager to support the new Nazi cultural
regime. When summoned to report for transport to the East,
he went into hiding. Coincidentally, he was brought to one of
the houses we had just passed on our way to The Hague. My
mother was staying there as well, and Boris, an overdressed
gay man, immediately took to my mother's great capacity
for tolerance and her passion for literature and music. This
passion was running wild and Boris had all his time available
to instruct my mother according to his strict rules.*

*When I started to think about the pieces of the puzzle
that brought all these people together in this house – of the
Russians, my mother and Boris – I began to develop a sense of
the intensity and drive these people used to keep their passions
alive, and of the equally passionate denial of the murderous
truth that was looking for them.*

*Soon they were thrown apart, and then brought together
again by organisations of resistance fighters that tried to keep
them safe. Both Boris and my mother grew emaciated and
finally lost the capacity to eat because hunger had damaged
their bodies. Neither of them ever touched the tulip bulbs
given to them as food. A flash of the fields we have just driven
through comes and goes in my mind, and is dismissed as
absurd. Flowers are to look at and smell, I remark rebelliously.*

Both smile and tell me I am right, but they had nothing else to eat. Boris doesn't say much. He is very old and sits by the stove, elegantly dressed in a bowtie and a dark red satin house jacket. There are sparse strands of perfumed hair on his skull. He turns to me and hums a croaky tune. Did I know that Tchaikovsky used this folk tune for one of his symphonies? he asks. He frightens me a little. I don't really know what he is talking about. My mother takes over and sings a few bars in her husky voice. 'That's the song mother sings to me at bedtime,' I say, relieved to be back on familiar ground. He nods and wipes his nearly blind eyes with an embroidered handkerchief.

He said that at the end of the war they often used to sing in the dark because they had nothing to provide light with.

I sing it to her: *moya radost*. I heard it being said to the children of a Russian friend, a poet, on a day in his garden near the sea, when we all listened to him playing the balalaika, a beautiful folk instrument, and mother was singing. My father had gone quiet. I could feel he was at the beginning of one of his episodes of dark, silent days when he would not speak to us. We walked together along the stately, old Dutch houses in the port of Veere, a seaside town in Zeeland, on the sea of uneasy cobblestones. The sky shone in a clean, clear manner, showing that there was nothing more to it, to our life, than this. Father and me holding hands, looking at the movement of the North Sea. He made me hop over one bollard then another. I jumped the chains in between them until we reached the end of the harbour and stood there with nowhere to go. We didn't speak. Father sighed, a vague yes, and I nodded in agreement. We turned around and I felt as if this bright and beautiful summer light had wiped out everything. We were just walking, seeing only a blank day around us. I filled in his silence with my own. That is how it started, me telling their story. With mother, so slender in her cotton dress, sitting under their mulberry tree full of fruit, singing, singing a folk tune.

She looks at me. Did she remember the mulberry tree at that Russian poet's place, I want to ask. It is one of these moments where time brings only one thought to two people; she starts to speak about that mulberry tree and also about the one in the South of France, in front of the house where for years we had spent our summers, when she was old and I had become a mother, with a daughter and a husband.

When in the heat of an afternoon we had all fallen asleep under the tree – woman, child, man, a nearly biblical small family close to the earth and the air – she stood over us and said that: *moya radost*, to the little one, to us. She was her mother, her grandmother, her great grandmother, all come back to tell us that we were her joy.

I am that traveller, a curious wanderer taking in what the world brings me, tells me. I find my way in the life I have to live through music and words, but also through nature and many, many conversations that I have along the road. I try to cultivate a personal, essential beauty I can drink from, so as to find a balance in what I hear about wars and children suffering, torture, the destruction of cultures never to be found again. I carry my family's history with me, making comparisons, of course, with the developments throughout the years. Always, I think of it as their story, not mine, until I start to see myself – and feel that others are seeing me – *through* their story, and until in fact their story *is* me.

Me, a singer, sitting in my hotel room in Sofia, the capital of Bulgaria.

I have been told that due to political circumstances there is no food available at the hotel, so my stomach is empty. This adds to the general feeling of bleakness that has already taken hold of me. By way of breakfast I have been served some salty hot water, a kind of greenish soup in a bowl I am now holding in my hands to keep myself a bit warm. It is mid-winter and very cold.

I am aware that I have some relatives in this city but I hesitate to contact them. I am here to give a concert and I don't feel in the right frame of mind because of that difficult connection with the memory of her, my aunt, who was married to this Bulgarian doctor and how, through their marriage, their family became my family.

This morning when I woke up and glanced out of the window I observed a strange scene. The image stays my mind and will not leave me.

The city is covered in snow. From my window I can see the clean, white square surrounded by heavy rococo buildings.

The scars that I notice in the otherwise spotless snow, seem to be paw prints and beside them, fainter, large shoe prints, clearly from a man's footwear. There is a neat line of red dots traced on the ground.

I get up from my chair and lean out of my window to take a closer look at those markings. In the corner of the square I see a man and a bear, a scraggy animal with a chain attached by a ring in his nose to his ear. The man is dressed in a thick, old coat. His shoes are red, as red as the blood that drips from the bear's nose when the man yanks at the chain to make him dance.

In the silent morning the bear dances to the rhythm of the man who shouts 'hop, hop' to accompany the animal's heavy task. I watch this joyless dance in front of his torturer and see no one to cheer him on.

Every now and then, when the man yanks the chain really hard, a drop of blood stains the snow. I grab my coat and hurry down the stairs. I forget my gloves and my hat. The cold hits my face as soon as I am outside. When I get closer to the animal, the man immediately holds out a mucky hand, and I understand that he is asking for coins. I reach in the pocket of my coat, and for a split second I nurture some absurd hope that I carry a gun with me. That I keep it there, in my deep coat pocket.

A gun. Why? I ask myself. I can't shoot and have no interest in weapons. I don't even know who it is I want to point that gun at, the man or the bear. The smell that comes off the bear's fur is foul. He looks me in the eye, tears of blood coming from his ear and his soft nose. He reminds me of one of these saints in medieval Italian paintings, formidable in his innocence and his suffering. The man also looks me in the eye. Hunger and the cold have made him a torturer. I think: *He has a reason to make this bear dance.*

It is then that I know my desire for a gun comes from a remote memory of some family history, something I had been told about as a child concerning one of my aunts, my mother's sister, the one who married this man from Sofia.

Back in my hotel room I close my eyes and I can again hear the voice of the person who told me this story, their flat, toneless manner.

Everybody used to turn around in the street when she walked past. She was a genuine beauty, with a kind smile, he told me.

I think I can hear the buzz of the jazz musicians and the conversations, the echo of the large halls or living spaces where she used to go to parties, the thumping of the heels while dancing, the broad laughter, and the hushed touch of the fine fabrics they all wore. I can picture her wearing a headband with a jewelled aigrette, her blonde hair cut short, a dress she embroidered herself with beads, Poiray style.

A very chic young woman, smoking her Egyptian cigarettes through a cigarette holder. She was soft-spoken and quite shy, which led to her being unable to refuse an offer to marry a man of great wealth and allure whom she did not love. While society approved of her marriage, her parents saw that she had got lost in herself, slipped away into loneliness. This led to a nervous breakdown after her decision to break up the short-lived union. But leaving her husband and getting a divorce at a very young age was frowned upon in her circles. Her parents advised her to go travelling in Europe, and visit friends until the rumours about her behaviour died down.

She settled somewhere on the Cote d'Azur. It was on a quiet day, when she was working in her friend's garden, that her host brought her the disturbing news about the imminent war. She smiled, hiding from the sun under the mimosa tree. She sniffed at a flower she had just picked and did not pay much attention to her host's news. She was still recovering and was trying to withdraw slightly from talk of news that might have an impact on her emotional balance. A moment later, though, when she made her way back to a house full of newly arrived visitors, she was introduced to a young Bulgarian and felt as if she had woken up from her state of stupor. They shook hands just a little too long and three months later they got married, on the day the Germans occupied France.

There was no going back to their respective homes, so they continued their travelling for three years. It wasn't the kind of travelling they did before they were branded as unwanted – it was forced travelling, fleeing from a growing threat of arrest, of being disposed of. T. had little contact with Holland. She heard via acquaintances that her parents, my grandparents, had died; that their houses had been confiscated by the Nazis and her brothers and sisters were either in Japanese camps in Indonesia or trying to evade arrest in Holland. There was no close family she felt she could call or write to. She spent those years in splendid isolation with her new husband, living in fear and luxury with various friends.

Her husband, who was a medical doctor, took risks by offering to work as a doctor for the resistance. Wounded men and women from the Maquis would be brought to him in the middle of the night, when he lived on some friend's estate in the mountains near Grenoble. His French was excellent and he still had his doctor's bag with him. Both he and my aunt were tall, blue-eyed, blonde creatures and even the members of the resistance found it hard to believe that they were Jews. They joked about it to the fair couple; but the conception of the 'Jewish look' is strangely, deeply engrained. Of course, France has long had a solid, bourgeois tradition of antisemitism. However, it is often claimed that the great French author Emile Zola even paid with his life for defending a Jewish individual he considered innocent, in the notorious Dreyfus affair. Maybe such ideas were just part of this tradition, but even these fierce anti-Nazi fighters harboured this misconception.

In December 1943 my aunt and uncle had a baby daughter.

When she was a week old their hosts lit a big fire in the main hall of their house and invited dignitaries and friends from the neighbouring town. Their wine cellar was still well filled and there were a lot of willing hands to help out with the party. It was well known in the region on which side these people stood, and people were prepared to make patés or provide sausages and cheeses for these friends. Bread was baked and there was music on that winter afternoon.

My aunt took her little baby out into the snowy garden, followed by the dogs. The Yellow House was built on the side of a mountain and from that garden the view of the Alps was spectacular. She must have taken a deep breath of mountain air, being outside with her baby, her husband safe inside the house surrounded by good people. Her clothes were still elegant, and she had so many. She was wearing a leopard skin fur, which by fluke came into my possession years later. She did realize that the threat of expulsion from this nest was always there. I think she must have felt a relative calm in herself. A new human being in her arms, the animals beside her in the snow, a horizon filled with protecting mountains.

After the war we learned never to harbour that kind of trust, that feeling of complete abandon to a happy, safe day. Not even for an hour.

Everybody present in the house knew the couple was there. None knew that they were Jews. The guests drank to the baby in the afternoon, they ate by the fire and left, satisfied with a good party. In the evening, the resistance fighters came to visit, they were a more intellectual crowd of Parisians who had fled to these mountains to fight the Germans. There were writers and painters among them.

The discussions that went on that night were not about the war at all. Books and films were criticized, they drank and laughed together and enjoyed the intimacy of their mutual camaraderie, until a latecomer brought bad news. There were some Boches, German soldiers, close by, searching houses for hidden Jews. My aunt and uncle looked at the man in his wet coat. Both of them felt he had brought the cold of winter with him, into the warm house.

'So,' my uncle said, 'we must go then, quickly, for the baby's sake as well.' Some of the men and women gathered showed surprise. 'We are yellow star people,' my uncle explained.

Immediate planning followed: how and where the resistance would take the couple and their baby. Instead of 'goodnight', they said 'pack'.

> *When I was in my twenties I travelled to these French mountains, to the Yellow House with the grand steps leading to the door in the monumental seventeenth century façade.*
>
> *I walked through the rooms and touched an object here and there. I walked in the garden with a pack of dogs at my heels and I took to the extreme beauty of the horizon. Members of the same family, who had been hosts to my relatives during the war, still lived there. They took me in. I sat by the light of a fire and let their stories about my family burn me, brand me.*

That morning the couple and child were smuggled by the resistance over the French Alps into Switzerland. However, they did not have the correct papers to take up residence there. They stayed at a pension and waited for their contact person to bring them documents that would allow them to stay in the country. My aunt, finally, wrote to my mother that she missed home. A letter that she addressed to close friends, went effortlessly from Switzerland to Holland and reached my mother within a month.

They had each other, my aunt and uncle. They bought Swiss life insurance and put money in a Swiss bank account. To build a life, that was the plan.

Soon it became apparent to their landlady that they had no papers, and she reported them to the Swiss authorities. Not until she had collected half a year's rent in advance from them, though.

The authorities decided to post them, just like that letter my aunt had sent home to her sister, over the Swiss-Austrian border. It was done effortlessly. In the afternoon they were arrested by the local police. And handed over. There were courteous exchanges between the Swiss police and the Austrian soldiers at the border.

The air was crisp with frost and the sky stretched over the snow-covered mountains in a lucid blue. The perfect day for a winter holiday. The soldiers joked with the couple as they urged them on. My aunt in her furs, holding the baby girl, my uncle in his long loden coat, helplessly trying to support his wife. They went past some farmhouses decorated with flowers and symbols of fertility, they walked past the well-polished open gates of an estate, they stumbled past a *Konditorei*, a typical Austrian café, and a *Bierkneipe*, a pub. The air was filled with such delicious smelling wood smoke, you'd nearly eat it. The soldiers continued bragging and joking among themselves.

Was it something my aunt said softly to her husband, about the nearby city of Lustenau being famous for its lace and embroidery, or how fond she was of Viennese waltzes, in an effort to remain herself: stylish and conversational at all cost?

There was a thick layer of snow on the field they tramped through. The sun hit the frozen path with thousands of ice-stars. The soldiers heard my aunt and told them to halt right there. Dance all you like, they told them. They made my uncle hold my tiny cousin, and they told them both to dance. Then they told the Bulgarian to dance on his own. What about some Bulgarian bear dance, did they not do something like that in his country? They shouted at him. 'Be a bear,' they shouted, 'be a bear.'

They had no reason to make him dance.

My aunt kept watching him, in agony, until the soldiers seemed to get bored and suddenly decided to bend the rules and go for a beer before taking them to the train station and sending them off to a camp. They went back to the *Kneipe* and ordered the couple to sit in the back while they had a few beers. There were some other people in the bar. They all quickly joined in with the soldiers' singing, except for a young woman at the back, where my aunt and uncle had been told to wait.

There was a back door. My uncle picked up the baby and hissed at my aunt to wait for a minute and then follow him outside. Before she understood what he was doing, he was gone. Outside to where? She panicked. To nowhere, to the snow, the hope for freedom, the adrenaline of a possible escape.

There were large windows in the café and one of the soldiers saw my uncle and ran after him while shouting at the others to follow him. The young woman at the back of the bar came up to my aunt and held her hand while they watched through the window, watched her husband, holding their child, dancing again like a bear. Until they shot him, and he dropped the child and fell on top of her. A soundless fall, a few drops of blood in the snow. They left them lying in the field like abandoned toys.

The soldiers came back in to make a phone call and arrange for some paperwork to be done as one prisoner was down. They had to report; all had to be in order. *Ordnung*.

In a hushed tone, the young woman beside her had told my aunt to leave, to run into the gates of the estate she had just walked past. Did she remember? She did as she was told while the soldiers were still outside. When they came inside the woman went to find the baby under the corpse of my uncle in the snow. Not a sound came from the child but it was alive. With the baby under her coat she ran back to her estate.

My aunt found herself sitting in an Austrian kitchen, completely calm. She introduced herself, gave her saviour her family details in Holland and told her what had happened to her. She must have been in such a state of shock that she momentarily thought herself to be back in the safe house in France, which was similar to this Austrian one. Her saviour took her to a bedroom and helped her undress.

Some soldiers came looking for them later that afternoon. The baby was asleep in her cot in the nursery where two other children were playing. When asked if she had come across a woman with a baby, the lady of the house told them coldly that she took no interest in the rabble that passed her gates every day. They clicked their heels, intimidated, and left.

My aunt woke up to hear German being spoken all around her. Quietly, in her embroidered nightgown, she went through the corridors only to encounter the woman who saved her the day before. A trembling panic paralyzed her. She wanted to speak, but no words came. No voice. The woman gently brought her to see her baby, but she did not react.

For months that family looked after her and my cousin. My aunt started speaking again, very softly, but only to ask about daily matters, the weather and food.

She liked spending all hours of the day in the stables, looking after the horses and the cows. Occasionally the stable boys heard her murmur to the animals in a language they did not understand.

When the war ended, her saviour contacted my mother, and my aunt and her child went back to Holland. The day she left Austria they handed her the toddler. She asked why she had to bring that child. When they told her the child was her daughter she laughed and shook her head. She had lost her mind.

My mother had a photograph on her desk of an elegant young woman, short blonde hair combed backwards *à la garconne*, soft wide eyes and an impeccable face. The face of my aunt.

She is so quiet, my aunt, always veiled in the smoke of her cigarettes, a crippled face, her long fingers manufacturing dresses and baubles for our dolls.

The tiny flower embroidering made me dream as a child. The dresses were like miniature ball gowns, open lace, a palette of pale silk in the embroidery. They were far too beautiful to put on anything. I stared endlessly at her gifts and told myself stories about them.

My aunt lived in a large nursing home in a park with tall trees. We would drive out to collect her from there every second weekend. We knew that she was unhappy, that was why she lived in a place for unhappy people.

The unhappy people made exciting furniture. We had a lot of this unhappy furniture as I called it. It was very nicely made handicraft work. My aunt sat in silence in the workshop at the home and made beautiful pieces, the way she made our dolls' dresses. My mother told me she had always been interested in making things, ever since she was small. 'But then,' my mother would smile her naughty smile, 'she also liked to live the high life, dress up, dance and socialize.'

Soon after the war, my aunt spent a few months with my mother, who had not yet met my father then. She smoked and ignored her child. She tore up the few photographs my mother had left from their family and set fire to them in their living room. My mother contacted the Bulgarian family of her murdered husband. They came and took the child with them, back to Sofia.

Always unexpectedly he would come to the back door of our house in Bergen aan Zee and knock. I would see his broad hat through the top window panes and jump up. I loved Grandfather W., as we used to call him, the Bulgarian who came with news of our cousin. He was her grandfather, not ours, but we did not have one and he played the part to perfection. Just not often enough.

He was guilty of making me believe that smuggling goods was for the benefit of mankind, or at least for us. He managed to bribe his way through communist borders and back at least three times a year and always arrived with bags full of presents. He was a medical doctor like his son, but had become a powerful business man. We loved, my sister and I, the silk blouses and the brightly coloured wooden boxes he gave us.

He drank jenever with my parents in the evening, while my mother smoked through the long, ornate cigarette holders that he brought her. His English was quite good, but he mainly spoke Russian with my mother. The first word I learned in Russian was *woyna*, war. They must have mentioned it a lot.

Once, they met in our house, my aunt and her father-in-law. He spoke to her bent head. His kind words about her child went unanswered. After a few minutes she lifted her blank eyes to him and said: 'Yes, yes'. I was playing in the room with the boxes he had brought and I was listening as well. I thought how strange it was that she said something, words that had no meaning, just sound. A war stood in between my aunt and the way she had lived her alphabet. I began to understand that extreme suffering can take away one language and bring on another one, one without memory. Yes.

A FATHER. A WRITER

YOU WERE MY FATHER, Maurits Mok. You changed your name from Mozes to Maurits because you thought that Maurits sounded better. Less obvious alliteration and more modern maybe, you used to explain it to me with that slight, nearly hesitant smile. You were once, long before World War II, a successful poet and an autodidact. At fourteen your father took you out of school, much to the distress of your schoolmaster, and you had to work in an office for diamond traders, writing letters, business correspondence you would call it. It sounded out of place when you mentioned it. I could not imagine you being an office person. Your boss couldn't either. That man must have had some wisdom in him, when he wasn't weighing his precious stones. With rabbinical insight he told young Maurits to go learn some languages. He paid leading professors to teach the young boy German, French, Spanish and English, saying it would help him to write good letters for his business. Maurits got paid for a full-time job and only worked in the mornings. In the afternoons he learned languages or went to libraries and read. The books he couldn't take home with him, he learned by heart. His parents never knew about these goings-on.

After four or five years, the language lessons in the afternoon hours were replaced by Maurits spending that time writing in a café. When his first works were published his boss smiled, and when Maurits told him that he wanted to be a man of letters, he laughed and told him good luck. And so father settled in Amsterdam with his older sister Saar, who taught in a school and worked as a classical pianist as well. At that time, around 1935, a lot of German Jewish artists had come to seek refuge from the Nazi regime in Holland. My father's sister Saar moved in with the her lover, Leo Strauss, from Berlin. Leo and his two young sons met my aunt Saar at a concert where she performed music by Chopin. My father continued his life as a serious single man in literature. This meant, apart from reading and writing, sitting in cafés in the morning, afternoon or night and taking part in discussions and parties while drinking jenever. He had a brief fling with a German girl. She became pregnant and gave birth to a girl, my sister Elsa. My father officially adopted Elsa and raised her. He never married her mother.

There must have been a great deal of flirting and passionate affairs going on in these terribly chaotic times before the war. Uprooted artists, with no money and often with no place where they could work, flung themselves into the bohemian life of Amsterdam. The gentlemen Tuschinski and Krasnapolsky had their big hotels and theatres at the disposition of those looking for distraction in a perfect Art Deco setting.

My father met the Jewish Austrian writer Joseph Roth, who was to become world famous years after his death. He was miserable, a heavy drinker and stranded in Amsterdam, penniless. His work and erudition fascinated my father and Roth became his mentor.

'You are a poet who drinks coffee,' Joseph Roth the famous alcoholic laughed at my father when he ordered coffee for breakfast during a meeting with him. I don't know how many times my father told me this story, even when I was a little girl. How Joseph Roth had large glasses of Burgundy for breakfast while remaining perfectly sober. And my father got more and more wound-up by the coffee and the excitement of discussing German literature and the very oppressive political developments in Germany. Roth had been writing a column in Berlin and was getting increasingly depressed by the rise of the Nazi party.

It is winter in New York. I kick at the hardened snow patches on my way to my favourite café Sabarsky, where they have a Steinway grand piano and serve Viennese strudel beside the

open fire, where I like to open my notebook on the wooden
table and lean back in the cushions, savouring the timeless
goings-on. It is there where I live in New York, with my
beloved friends just a telephone call away. Where, so often,
I seem to recognize faces out in the street. Where I know my
family would have lived. Where I look at the scores for my
next rehearsal and look up through the tall windows to watch
the passers-by find their way through a maze of snowflakes.
And then I dream of them coming in to say hi. It could be an
annoying aunt with noisy children, and we could complain to
each other about this or that. Life. When I have my fill of cake
I go upstairs to the Neue Galerie museum bookshop see if they
have any new books. There it is: a book called Joseph Roth: A
Life in Letters. *I open the book right there, and see a picture of*
Joseph and my father and some artist friends of theirs, sitting
in a café in Amsterdam in 1937. That is how my father came
to greet me that day in New York.

Joseph Roth encouraged my father as a writer and by the late
thirties his name was well established. Established enough for him to
write a pamphlet addressed to the nation, warning people about the
rise of antisemitism and the threat of a war with Germany, and to be
taken seriously by a large number of readers.

One day in Amsterdam I receive a phone call from a close
friend. 'We have bought a house, come and see it.' I go, her
wish is my command. We drive up a dune, we go up a number
of steps and she opens the door to the large old house. Her
new house. I stand in the hallway and, as if driven by a dream,
I go down the stairs. The door to a room is open. The room
is empty. There is one large window filled with summer green.
And one large cupboard built into the wall that turns out to
be a safe. I feel warm and sheltered in the embrace of this
room, but I want to close the safe shut, to lock away whatever

threat I feel. My friend comes in brandishing a booklet. It is
a short history of the house, which, as it turns out, used to
be owned by Henriette Roland Holst, a formidable poet and
communist from a wealthy background who was a respected
patron of the arts. She took my father under her wing when
he was nineteen and encouraged him in his work. Years later,
at the end of the 1930s he moved into this downstairs room.
The one I am standing in. I must have felt a remainder of his
presence. I move around the room hoping for more, a shadow,
a scratch of a pencil. Nothing. It moves me that my friends live
here now and that I will be able to stay with them, in the room
where my father lived and wrote his famous pamphlet about
the rise of the Nazis and their plans for the extermination of
the Jewish people.

In 1939 my father sat down at his desk in this window and wrote
his pamphlet about the situation in Europe, and Germany in particular.
How Jews were being killed already, and would be exterminated in
the coming years. A prophetic pamphlet. How many people read it? I
wonder. How few believed him, I know.

I stay in the room and try to be my own father held between
the walls of this quiet place.

A nervous fear must have driven him to write quickly, against
time, against a shattering wave of dark news that he could not ignore;
against his hope that none of this would come to pass and he would,
for long years to come, be able to take the short train ride to his
parents, like on that beautiful evening.

He would often tell me to look up: cloud formations hiding the fire
of the sun, spreading, pink, purple, orange clashes in his evening sky.
The one that was always there for him.

It must have been such an evening when he went to see his parents,
who by then lived on the seashore in Zandvoort. They, together with

his sister Saar and her companion Leo, would break bread at table and try to behave as if the familiar rituals of their meal would continue till the end of their peaceful lives. Maurits looked at them, watched their hands move, held his breath as if to freeze their movements. And then, a few months later when the soldiers' boots echoed along their street, he spilled it all out by telling them to go hide, flee. And his father joking, looking at his artistic children in happy dismay and uncomfortable disbelief.

And still Maurits devoted himself to poetry, and Saar to her piano. They laughed with their poet, painter and musician friends and played at bohemian life during long, late nights. No yellow star ever shone on their clothes when they left at the end of a party, to go into a menacing night occupied by Germans. They went on like this until all doors closed to them and they were forced to go into hiding or obey the German orders to board the trains to the camps.

It became hiding. Hiding from daylight, and spying eyes. Hiding from books and music. Hiding away with your family, at the mercy of mostly well-meaning courageous people, with whom they had nothing in common but fear.

I sat with him in the living room of his last home, back in Bergen where I was born. We sat, both reading. When I looked up from my book I saw the sweat on his face. It was not warm in the room and I was worried about the old man. It was a memory that had made him sweat with angst, he said. It was that couple of gay women who were hiding him in their attic, he said. I knew one of them had offered to marry him. A mixed marriage would make him less vulnerable to the Nazi regime for a short period. He accepted and married her. Grateful for her offer, he wanted to do as much as he could for her and her girlfriend. It was 1944, when he had lost contact with his daughter, when he knew already that his parents and sister had been put on a transport to the camps, that the two women started to demand that he go out into the world and buy drugs for them. They threatened to hand him over to the Gestapo if he refused. They were heavily addicted to opiates and Maurits knew doctors in the resistance.

He sat in a train full of soldiers, he said. On a sunny day. He was wearing a hat and reading a newspaper, blanking out all thoughts of danger. He went to Amsterdam from Hilversum and met up with his writer friends who had founded an underground publishing house, De Bezige Bij. Later, after the war, it became one of the most outstanding publishing houses in Holland. He handed in his critical stories and poems, to be published under his fake name – Hector Mantinga – and went on his way to find drugs for the women who sheltered him and tortured him as well.

This I only learned very recently, when I received a message on the internet from an unknown person, who had been a neighbour of my father's 'war wife' and her partner. It turned out that she and her girlfriend were jailed after the war for the extortion and blackmail of the Jewish people they seemed to be helping.

He managed to escape these women's house and found shelter at a fellow writer's place till the end of the war. But he never mentioned this blackmail to us. Too much pressure and fear take on a life of their own, he said. He let this memory loose, let it wander ... until it came back to visit him and me, and darkened the soft light of an afternoon in Bergen – where he still did not tell me about it. We sat together, with angst that was to be relived again.

When the war was over, he was given coupons to survive, to put clothes on his back. He bought the shiny green fabric that later so horrified my mother, and had a suit made from it. He bounced back into life like a fresh apple, he often joked. That reluctant, but sweet smile on his face.

Life, yes, all went back to normal, the clockwork of Holland had been reset. It was as if the history of the occupation, and the liquidation of more than a hundred thousand people needed to be framed and put away. The postman cycled around and brought envelopes full of news.

The Red Cross regretfully informed him of the death of his sister Saar Mok in the concentration camp of Auschwitz, but could not tell him anything about his parents. Queen Wilhelmina invited him for tea. He went in his shiny suit and she told him that she admired his work, and how reading his poems had given her support during those dreadful past years. On her writing desk there was a framed poem of his. After that visit, the yearly envelope would arrive from the royals with an 'honarary' financial contribution. Friends and admirers wrote to him. He read the letters in the garage where he was living and working, and felt the growing urge to know what exactly had happened to his parents. He had nothing to hold on to, not even an envelope containing devastating news.

Although I knew him as a person who was clinging to the mysticism of the real world that he inhabited, back then he seems to have reached out to the world of spirits and called on the famous clairvoyant Gerard Croiset to get closure about his loved ones. He told me that the moment he set foot in Croiset's office, the clairvoyant said that they were dead. He refused to give my father details of what he described as their 'horrendous' suffering. With this information my father stepped out into the afternoon, walked through the city of Amsterdam to Centraal Station and took the train back home to his garage. He sat down and started writing about the ghosts that were now his family. Two years later he met my mother and they married.

My mother was suffering from tuberculosis and was forced to rest at home. It took some planning to get her over to the registery office in Laren where they were to be married. A select crowd of friends, and their witnesses, were waiting for them in the hall. As the mayor opened the register so my parents could sign in their union, it turned out that my father was still married to the woman who had offered him protection during the war and later blackmailed him. There was some laughter, and the marriage was postponed for a couple of months.

When they finally got married my mother was still ill. There is only one photograph of my parents' wedding. My mother is lying on her bed in a pre-war designer dress with my father sitting beside her, surrounded by four friends. All of them are sitting on her bed holding glasses. I hope they drank champagne. Nobody ever told me. Although my parents were nearly middle-aged they seem like young people with a strong look in their eyes.

Once my mother was allowed to leave her sick bed, she became pregnant. My sister was born in the hospital in Laren. They were still living in the refurbished garage, but my father's patron the poet Adriaan Roland Holst, nephew of my father's former patron Henriette, who also lived in Laren, suggested that my father take a trip to Bergen, where he himself intended to live. He brought more or less the entire Laren community of artists with him, and that meant that my parents should move there as well.

Together they travelled to Bergen in his car, had lunch at a café called Het Huis Met De Pilaren and looked around the village for houses they could live in. My father wanted to be near the sea, so they drove the six kilometres through the woods and dunes to Bergen aan Zee, part of the municipality of Bergen. The closer they came to the seashore, the more my father seemed enchanted by the light around them. He later called it *zeelicht*, 'sealight', in his poems and it became a new word in the Dutch vocabulary. Maybe, when he stood on a sand dune overlooking a small patch of woodland and a long stretch of dunes, he felt that more words would come to him in this tiny village on the sea. He told his friend Adriaan that he was going to build a house across the road. His pockets were empty, but he was determined. Back in Bergen they met up with some artist friends and drank to the new inhabitants.

The architect Gerrit Rietveld was contacted by my father's friends, and a pupil of this famous man designed a house for our family.

When the house was finished, my father and Adriaan Roland Holst drove over to the village again, and were shown around the modern and bright house that would be my place of birth. When asked how he was hoping to pay for the house, my father shrugged, laughed, and pulled the torn pockets out of his trousers. He found a ten cents coin and gave it to the architect. But the man gave it back to him. The house was already paid for. An admirer of my father's work, an extremely wealthy Jewish man, had taken care of it. He would continue to look after him by regularly sending cheques. At that time the German state's reparations and war foundations were not yet in operation and surviving Jews were often left completely without means.

When my father was reading from his work or being inteviewed on the radio, we had to sit and be very quiet, showing respect for his work. I did not understand his work at all, but I did not mind listening to the sound of his deep voice. Often there were visitors who listened in with us. My father's close friend the painter and sculptor Geertjan van Meurs came walking along the beach from the next village with his dog and stayed to talk about philosophy or literature while drinking jenever. These men could swear and shout about subjects that went completely over our heads. We snatched olives and pickles from the table while they were drinking. My mother liked to throw in a quote, always raising her voice as she did so, as if to secure her position on an equal intellectual level in this competitive family.

In the long hours in which we climbed trees, got our socks wet during cold winter months when we still ventured into the sea, hopped from one bale of hay to the next until the stable owner came after us, went skating from the windmill to the hot chocolate stands on the ice, trained in our ballet or music classes, fell in and out of love with insufferable boys, ripped our knees open, stood in front of the long hall mirror dressed up in velvet, lace and hats, shouted at each other in Russian pretending to be politicians, in these long hours my father worked. He wrote poems about us and poems about them, the ones who were gone.

His friends, and some of my mother's – who came to share food, songs, talks and summer evenings bathing in the calm sea – were living with the heavy traumas of their past. But somehow my father managed to make me see them for who they were, rather than what they represented. Lydia, who took me to fashion shows where she worked as a model. Lydia who always wore long sleeved garments so as not to show the number on her arm. This young woman, who together with her sister had been experimented on by Dr Mengele in a camp, had come back to Holland alone. To me this woman was just a shining beauty, who went through life with a light step, well-dressed. She gave me a Siamese kitten. She had lots of cats instead of children. For children you needed a womb, and her womb was buried in a camp. Nobody mentioned this to us, of course.

We watched Mr Brent ride by on his bicycle, sitting erect, his bushy hair blowing about. My father commented that he looked like a true Spanish Grandee. A Sephardic Jew, the eminent scholar Brent was alone, always alone with the wind blowing through him, blowing through his hair. To us he was a wise and clever Spanish nobleman who told us fascinating stories. To others he was a lonely man striving to live his ruined life.

Men and women at the house of our early youth: we only knew them for their paintings, their books or other outstanding talents. My father managed to make them leave their ghosts at the front door and live with us children for a while.

Father sings when he shaves. Little bits of classical stuff, Bach is probably his favourite. One day he tells us that he wrote an essay about the composer Bach for a prominent literary magazine, and he insists that we read it. And then he talks about Bach on the radio. He turns it on after dinner, the plates are still on the table. In a kind of religious silence we listen to father talking about Bach on a clear spring evening. I sit there thinking that a lot of complicated words seem to be needed when expressing your thoughts about Bach, and also: When will I be allowed to go outside and do the double skipping rope jumping with my neighbour friend? I decide I prefer Bach when Father sings it to himself in the morning. When the piece is over, both our parents come outside and Father turns the ropes for us and even attempts to jump. I forgive him the difficult minutes of Bach.

Every year he takes us to listen to Bach's *St Matthew Passion*, the Concertgebouw performance. I get to wear my favourite dress and shoes and I succumb to the music without being bored for a second. I wanted to do my father a favour by being attentive, but I soon realize he has done me a favour by bringing me. I can hear the expression of pain in the music, I can relate to it as my father's.

On the way home from Amsterdam, back to our seaside village, we always stop to buy *kroketten*, the typical Dutch meat-filled croquettes. While my sister and I devour these dubious delicacies, my parents, secretly enjoying their croquettes too, talk about the performance and about the people they met at the concert. I think it perfectly normal that Father was asked to sign one of his books by the conductor, that at the break we went to the artists' foyer and talked to people who seemed to respect my parents. It makes me feel proud of them.

Often, down through the years, when I wake up in different countries that I find to be, for the time being, my home, I think I can hear father's deep voice coming from the bathroom. 'Mache dich, mein Herze, rein', make yourself pure, my heart. A bass aria accompanied by the buzz of an electric shaver.

Sometimes I think of his serious wish to see me on the stage of the Concertgebouw after I had announced, with the aplomb of a voracious teenager, that I was going to be a singer. I made it. Step by step I came down those long stairs for the first time, with my father sitting there in the audience, and I stood in front of the orchestra in an opulent dress and sang. Afterwards, his eyes shone.

All the happy songs in his life, I cherish.

The times in the South of France when my mother danced herself off her feet with some local beau, and my father and his artist friends, and many others, sat and talked philosophy to a wide range of wine bottles. Philosophy that ended in them singing some song, '*Mackie Messer*', Mack the Knife, along the road down the mountain. A song interrupted by laughter and donkeys braying, and perhaps a moment of sobering up, only for it to start again, sung arm in arm with friends, booming to the rising southern sun, the wild flowers we waded

through, the festive butterflies, until the *Haifisch,* the shark, lost its
teeth and we all fell asleep in a house full of open windows. Late at
night and early in the morning, we were there and allowed to share the
merriment of the big children. Those Bertolt Brecht lyrics were often dug up again. Much later in
Amsterdam in the company of visiting German poets, the Vondelpark
would resonate with their alcohol-fuelled songs. Or after dinner, father
would do his impersonation of Marlene Dietrich, a great favourite of
his. With his slender posture, crowned by an unlikely mass of grey
hair, clad in his tweed jacket, his pronounced features focused into
a perfomer's pout, he would proclaim in a half-sung manner that he
was 'made of love from head to toe'. This would be accompanied by
deafening laughter.

During the last six months of his life, he refused to go into his
work room claiming that 'they' were waiting for him. Time and again
he asked me could I not see them. They were telling him something,
he said. He was so frail, I did not want to offend him, so I asked what
he thought they were telling him. He sat in his modern living room,
on his Swedish designer chair surrounded by light, and started to cry.

I had rarely heard him cry and tried to take his hand. It was
resting on an open book by Paul Celan. I wondered briefly why he was
rereading this great poet's work. We had recently met his friend and
fellow poet the French author Edmond Jabès, who told Father and me
stories about the last terrifying years of Celan's existence.

He started to hum a song, a Yiddish song, only to stop abruptly. It
was his sister Saar's birthday he said, she liked this song, they used to
sing it together. *Mit raisinken und mandeln* ... he started it up again.
Now I was crying. He had never mentioned this fact before and I
had never heard him sing a song in Yiddish. It was for her he said,
and he started this haunting tune again. Then he got up and opened
the door to his workroom, but he didn't go inside. Instead he turned
around and asked me if it was too late to go? Where? I asked through
my tears. All these years of unbroken silence waiting for this song to
come back. Where? I asked again. To Auschwitz, to erect a monument

for his sister Saar. Auschwitz, the place where she was murdered, her and her music. He sang again, shaking. He seemed to hope that, I, his child, could make this happen. There was nothing I could do except share his suffering. He never had the courage to sing this song after her death. It had been replaced by the songs of his new life. I gathered half a century of unsung pain into myself.

Today, he said, she had asked for it. His voice was so weak when he asked me if I thought that 'they', the ones who were waiting for him in his workroom, could hear him.

A week later he died.

My teacher is that great soprano, a diva who joined the Nazi party to promote her career and took a Nazi lover. The great artist who makes me an interpreter of all those composers that were the backbone of my parents and grandparents' evenings, either at home or in a concert hall. She touches my face and my body to sharpen my vocal technique and she asks me how I hear music. She tells me to go home and think about it. I do, not realizing at the time that she had once been a happy Nazi. Icons are untouchable when they master great art.

In that night, I sit with a volume of my father's poems and I read a poem about his family. I then think it must be poor cousin Aal whose music I hear; I think about how it colours the sound of my voice.

In one of his poems, the lamp is lit. A soft light shines on his mother's hands and the hands of their gentle cousin. Aal, she was called. At that time in his life his name was still Mozes. The time when he used to come home from school in the afternoon and his mother would be sewing at the round table. His sister Saar would be studying at her desk and cousin Aal would jump up when she saw little Mozes and hug him warmly. His life was round then. The hours marked by habits. The maid's knock on the door, her rattling in with the teacups on the tray at four in the afternoon. Those cups his mother was so proud of. She had brought them with her dowry. Limoges porcelain, white, with drooping roses. His mother's voice reprimanding their maid, she had to be careful, every day, mother said, every day, the same. The trustworthy Leah, their maid, was pretty and very young. Her hands were small and her lips full and red. She giggled a lot. She giggled all the time when cousin Aal came for her monthly stay and spent most of her day sitting at the kitchen table. Playing her music. Did Mozes want to hear her play a new piece, she would ask. When he was a toddler he was afraid of Aal, because of the incessant drumming of all of her ten fat fingers on the table and the way she shouted at him, asking him in her loud voice if he liked her music. He would hide behind his father. His father, who stroked his head and told him not to be afraid of her, that Aal was an innocent being. '*Stumm, sei stumm*,' he whispered in his son's ear. She was a young adult when he was a small boy. Brain damaged at birth, she was mentally well enough to live with her family and even spend time with relatives now and then.

Her fingers never stopped moving and Mozes got used to her silent music, the one she imagined they all could hear and enjoy.

When his sister Saar played the piano in the living room, Aal would go quiet and sometimes cry. Her face wet with tears, she told them that Saar stole her music. Then Leah would take her out for a walk around Haarlem. And inevitably Aal would come back with a small present for her cousin Mozes, because he was a good boy and did not play her music.

After a few years, the mystery and strangeness of cousin Aal and her imaginary music became another comfortable normality in his life. The vision of her broad-backed figure spilling over the kitchen chair when she was frantically performing was part of the pattern of his days. Something like his father's hat, which he hung on the same hook every evening, leaving a deepening stain on the wall.

When, as a young man, he started writing poetry and broke out of this world and its comforting familiarity, he often thought about his cousin's dumb music. And those two young women, Leah and Aal, in their hats and long cloaks peering in the shop windows of their small city of Haarlem; Leah taking her to the market and coming home to tell everybody who wanted to hear it that Aal liked dates and apricots, and dried figs. And then she giggled, a high giggle. Beautiful Leah with her white apron and narrow wrists. The long, long mane of her dark curls on her back when she went out with her betrothed. How Mozes, as a young boy, had wanted to go to sleep entangled in that hair. Leah got married and had a baby, Miriam, who grew up just as slender and lovely as her mother and who, with some help from the family, studied German and became a translator. Miriam came to work for his parents long after Mozes had left for Amsterdam to become a well-known poet.

It was Miriam who brought cousin Aal for a visit to Leah's house. Aal played for Leah and Miriam on the kitchen table before they got arrested. The three women were put on the train to the concentration camp together. On the train Aal complained that she had no space. She complained to the soldiers when they arrived at the camp and they laughed and joked and asked her what she needed space for. For her music of course, she told them.

In 1945 Leah came back alone, bald and broken, to tell Mozes, who was now called Maurits, about them. She took his arm when they went to visit his parents' house. Other people with normal lives were living there now. When they answered the doorbell they were hesitant to let these strange Jews in. He wanted to look at the stain on the wall. The shadow of his father's hat. Just that.

He listened to Leah telling him how, in the camp, the brutes had been amused by cousin Aal's innocence. How they kept her for a few weeks as a wind-up puppet and made her play on the table in the canteen. How Aal stopped talking to her. How Aal finally told her in her noisy way that Miriam was sitting on the soldiers' knees, naked. That she had told them Miriam had to get dressed to listen to her. That she could not play anymore. The next morning, Aal was called up to be killed. The women embraced. I can hear it, Aal told her, and she kept asking her if Leah could hear it as well. The music.

Maurits embraced Leah and walked her to her bus. He then cycled home and wrote about the light of the lamp, a soft memory of his parents' hands come back to shine.

New friends, old souls, angels ...

I was a child and I knew nothing about other people. I made friends with my parents' friends. I made friends with these old people whose age meant nothing to me. They were small in size, they talked and talked around my ears, their stories were full of smiles and tears, their throats full of songs. Katia and Jaap were 'my good aunt and uncle'. Not official members of my family but I thought of them as such, as the Good Ones who would help me fly if I wanted to ...

Back then, when cruel fairytales played through my head night and day, back then I had my new friends who knew them, and told me about them, the ones who lived in my parents' silence ... and how I would, possibly, never be able to understand about the world or people, but maybe to try loving them a little bit all the same.

KATIA

I AM AT the house with the thatched roof where 'aunt' Katia my mother's friend lives. We drove from the seaside to the sandy plains to see the heather bloom and stay at the house of Katia.

Aged six I sit in the dark-panelled living room and look through books with extraordinary images. Fairytale figures in heavily ornate clothes and jewellery, the yellows and reds and gold jump off the pages. I can't read the text because it's in Russian. I know the routine of the day: Mother and Katia talk in Russian in the kitchen. Their unfamiliar tones are mixed with laughter, and the scents of coffee and spices drift into the living room and wrap me in a feeling of slight discomfort. Before night falls they will start crying and wipe the fat tears off their cheeks with smiles. Apparently it is healthy to cry in Russian. To me, adults who cry must be in terrible pain. Such displays do not fit into the profoundly Calvinist society of Holland. But obviously, we don't fit in with that society. Katia was born into a Jewish family of intellectuals in Sarajevo. She rolls her 'r's when she speaks Dutch to me. She seems like the epitome of the fairy godmother, her heavily lined face is always smiling, and whatever plan I come up with, she agrees to make it happen. Her eyes are dark and strong and I think she knows the solution to all the mysteries in life. When she was growing up, it was a free and forward-looking world in Yugoslavia that enabled her to study as a young woman, and to become a scholar of Russian and Serbo-Croat languages. Her ideals about an equality-based society brought her to have a brief flirtation with communism, during which she decided to travel to Moscow. In the city of the future, as the new young communists like to call it, Katia became a professor at a university there and, though mainly mixing with Russian poets, she met and fell in love with an idealistic Dutch architect. While her lover travelled to spread new ideas throughout Russia, Katia taught eager working class students and gave birth to a baby boy. When her lover returned, he did not seem pleased with the baby. He did continue to grace her with his presence, and he lived in her apartment until World War II broke out. When he decided it was time to return to his native land, Holland, Katia, who was pregnant again, came along. Family and friends turned away from the exuberant dark-haired woman, and her husband, as he now was, demanded that she parade her pregnant belly and Jewishness on the other side of the street whenever they were out together. She left him and, with her two small sons, found a hiding place with a Dutch family during the rest of the war. After the war, for her there was no going back to Sarajevo. With that smile, which deepened over the years that I knew her, she would shake her head at me and ask what she could have gone back to. I had no answer to that. I listened to her melodious voice with intense pleasure when, again and again, she expressed her love for her sons.

You can never love enough was her leitmotif, it resounded in her life. In mine.

After a copious lunch, my mother and Katia would sit down and discuss newly read books and I was allowed to wander down the street. It was a dead-end street with only a couple of houses on it. The buildings were mainly hidden by hydrangeas and rhododendrons, plants that I would later consider to be the serious kind of flora necessary to the gardens of the solid Dutch bourgeois.

I knew none of the inhabitants of these places. They kept their distance from my aunt Katia's slightly bohemian household and her emotional visitors. I followed the street down to where a large barrier blocked off the fields full of purple heather. There, for some reason still inexplicable to me, I stood for at least half an hour caught up in dreams and thoughts. The facts that I had been told about my beloved Katia had shaped themselves into a ball of anger in my head and I considered she had been wronged by life. To clear the bad, as I called it to my child self, was my mission. The purple, stubborn little flowers of the heather gave off a heavy sugary scent. Bees and butterflies took the pollen and nature seemed generous and wonderful to me. If it wasn't for that bad, all would have fitted calmly in my world. I leaned on a fence and looked out over the fields as if to find something written, and my head was full of cloud-like, unshaped words. Then, after about half an hour, I turned back to have tea and cake.

Katia baked great cakes with chocolate and seeds. After tea we would walk to the village centre and I was allowed to chose my favourite food for dinner. Sometimes Katia or my mother made me pronounce the name of certain vegetables or fruit in Russian, so I could learn the language while eating, they joked. We certainly did a lot of eating. And talking and laughing as well. With that tinge of a melancholy undertone to it all. They thought I couldn't hear it. But I did. Like I heard their crying and singing over the glasses of wine and *slivovitz* after dinner, when I was tucked away in my cosy bed with borrowed ancient teddybears on it. A weightless down covered me and the strange toys kept me awake, as well as their songs. I hummed along with the Balkan *lieder* and the words were marked down in my brain. '*Ni što mene bole da so samo serše rana*', nobody knows how my heart hurts. They were love songs, songs from life.

JAAP

WHEN THE RED berries appear on the rowan trees, they trigger my memory of him. Mr Hemelrijk. Literally translated, his name means Kingdom of Heaven. For me he was always a king. A king, and a child just like me. We were friends, we'd walk to the end of his garden and he'd open the small wooden gate that led to the abandoned train tracks in the dunes. We'd walk down the sandy road and he'd hold my hand in his. Sometimes we did not even speak. I was four years old when he asked me what I thought of the world. I looked at his tanned hand and then I looked up into his large dark eyes. He always smiled at me with a deep sadness. A warm sadness. The world had only one brilliant colour for me then. And I think he liked to share this unity with me.

In late summer, we used to cycle through the woods from our house to his house. The dark, sweet smell of honeysuckle all along the road. I sat on the back of my father's bicycle and held some book or other that they were surely going to discuss. I knew the routine when we arrived. Mr Hemelrijk stood on the terrace at the front of his large house and waited for us. As soon as he saw us he would rush to one of the gates, there were two, and welcome us with great warmth and enthusiasm, as if he had not seen us in months. In fact, he used to cycle to our house on the seashore every evening for a swim, and a drink on our terrace. He led my parents through the open doors into his large study as I went to the back of the house to get my treat in the kitchen. I was allowed to bring my drink into the study and listen to their conversation for a while, until I got bored and went to the swings or the attic full of games and toys.

I loved his modern study. Grey carpeted floors, Bauhaus furniture, a large, tidy desk and books, books everywhere. I was wrapped in pipe and cigarette smoke and felt comforted by it. Before I could read I had looked at his family photographs. He seemed to have a large number of brothers and sisters. I half-listened to the conversations about men called Proust or Musil, and wandered off into the monumental hallway.

But I was a curious child. I remember the day when I asked him about his family before I left the room. Did they all live in such a beautiful house? I wanted to know. Did they all teach stories like him, the ancient Greek stories, were they all good swimmers like him? That's when he said he would take me out for a walk later and tell me about them. That is how our walks started.

Jaap Hemelrijk was like a brother to my father, although he was a great deal older than him and was already a grandfather by the time he met my father. In fact two of his granddaughters, who were teenagers when I was a small child, lived with him and his wife in that big house.

After the war he had acquired the status of principal of one of the leading *gymnasiums* in Holland, an elite school which he presided over like a wise rabbi.

I heard him talk about children and adults as if they were the same kind, with the same rights and wrongs, and I developed, or maybe over-developed, a sense of self-righteousness; a sense that I may be a child but I had a voice and a brain and should be heard as much as any adult.

And then, that day when I wandered into the large hallway with its double staircase, the phone rang. The phone was placed on a small table in a separate room. You could call it an indoor phone booth. I was impressed by the loud ringing through the house and the importance of a phone call. Mr Hemelrijk came out of the study, sat down in the booth and calmly lifted the receiver.

I dawdled, and through the milk-glass door, watched him bend over towards the black phone as if in pain. I just stood there, a little girl aware of the sand between my toes and the stickiness of my hands.

When he opened the door, I saw tears in his eyes. I followed him back into the study and heard him explain to my parents that some friend from the camps had died.

'Shush,' my father said, 'Judith.'

Yes, Judith was standing there. As I was when I stood in our large window at home overlooking the woods and heard my parents whisper about the camps. And at night I imagined shapes would slowly come to me and whisper. Angry whispers they were.

There was never any dust on the books in his library. He must have read them all the time, I thought. But I suppose he just liked to keep them clean and available. Literature in various languages and a whole section of books about World War II.

His bookcases were black and shiny and I would look at the books and think that the swastikas on the books matched the cases. A lot of those books were at my parents' house as well, but I was not allowed to read anything about the war until I was well into my teenage years.

He owned a blue sleigh decorated in gold leaf with the moon and stars. The sleigh seated four and had to be pulled by horses. It was parked beside the front door at the side of the house and made me dream. Whenever I asked him about it, he said it belonged to his sisters and they were gone.

They were gone ... A phrase I kept hearing at home, and now here. But I was here, I told him, and I wanted to ride in that sleigh. He laughed and kept quiet.

By the time I was six years old I went to a small school in the woods very close to his house and I visited him quite often. He sat in his study and we talked about what I had learned and liked.

Winter came with deep snow. He looked at it and told me how cold he had been in Mauthausen. Or was it another camp? He had been through four concentration camps and survived. The deep sadness he held in his eyes did not worry me, surely he would tell me about it, I thought. I was a confident, innocent child.

We sat in our classroom in the afternoon and heard the tinkle of many bells. Our neighbour from across the road, whose daughter was in my class, owned two thoroughbred horses. I saw them through our classroom window, in full attire, blankets tied on their back, strapped in blue and gold and pulling a blue and gold sleigh. The image faded in and out through a curtain of fine snow. We were allowed, my friend and I, to pull on our coats and hats and rush out. Her father wrapped us in old furs and off we went through the dunes, past Mr Hemelrijk's house. We waved from his sleigh. Our neighbour had borrowed it for the occasion and I wished and wished that the trip would never end. The faint tinkle of the bells, the soft rhythm of the horse's hooves, the pure air and calm beauty of the pine forest. It did end: I came home and was fed, got a goodnight kiss and lay in bed listening to my father reading one of the new children's stories that he had written. Then in the dark, I started thinking of how Mr Hemelrijk must get his sleigh back, if only to remember his sisters. They were gone and he had been cold, he said. I lay awake thinking about this and pulled my warm blanket around me like a thick shadow.

As we continued with our walks and talks, I grew taller and he grew smaller.

Slowly, very slowly he fed me crumbs of his life story until, I think, I would be able to digest the entire ugly clump of it. He spared me without omitting the truth. He had a lot of paintings in his house. There were the ones of his wife wearing matching jewellery that I kept admiring. The strict hairdo and the necklace, rings and earrings. She taught me: onyx and gold, tiger's eye, lapis lazuli, platinum. I repeated them to myself when I listened to Mr Hemelrijk telling me about the artist whose work I was looking at. That artist came from the same town as Jaap Hemelrijk: Winterswijk.

Jaap had encouraged him to paint and introduced him to another well-known artist. Yes, he said and he stroked my hair and encouraged me to finish my cake. The room was warm with words and safety, and stories of a past that had been conquered with a passion. I ate my cake during the silence that seemed to fuel his memory, and then another story followed.

'This man became a well known artist, you know Judith, he painted a portrait of Theodor Herzl, the founder of Zionism,' he said. They had had parties at the house, right here where I was sitting, on this old sofa. Max with his dark head of hair, met Fré Cohen, pretty Fré, with her massive curls and her tiny body, so lovely, and so insistent about her ideals. 'See,' he points at a drawing, something hesistant in his gesture, 'that is Fré, a self-portrait.'

Busy little Fré, they used to call her. She was very lively and loved to dance. She would talk Max into socialist activities, women's rights and her big ideal: Zionism. Max laughed and danced with her, but he had his reservations about her ideals. She got him a lot of work though. My very old friend moves around the room, as if going from one friend to the next: these people he is telling me about, they are all still here with him. He manages to make me love the paintings just as much as he loves them.

There is a self-portrait of Max as well. I look at this face with its open expression. I read a resolute dedication to himself and his art in it. Something I can recognize even at my young age.

I asked Jaap Hemelrijk before he told me: Were they gone as well? He nodded.

Before I knew it Max and Fré had danced out of this nice room into a devouring darkness. What happened to these eager young friends when the Nazis occupied their country, my country? Max tried to flee to Switzerland but was arrested and sent back to Drancy in France. He continued to draw in the camp until he was brought to Sobibor. The Nazi officers greatly admired the skills of this little Jew and ordered him to paint their portraits. 'From Herzl to Himmler we could say,' says Mr Hemelrijk. It's the first time that I hear an edge to his voice. Not that Max painted Himmler, but some other piece of Nazi scum.

I closed my eyes on the self-portrait of Max, imagining him emaciated, his head exploding with memories, but just as determined to paint a good portrait of his murderers to be, as when he had painted the Zionist Herzl. And Fré Cohen, the talented artist who charmed him and many others into understanding women's rights, rights for artists and better social laws for the deprived. She used to stay at the new Bio Vakantieoord, a 'people's holiday home' organized by Holland's foremost progressive politician. The building in the seashore village of Egmond aan Zee has his name.

When, in my teenage years we would stay at our flat there, on the seashore with my parents, I would let myself be pushed by the northern gale along the boulevard, the sea wild and indifferent at my left, the empty holiday homes clinging to the sand dunes at my right, past that big building, the holiday home, its emptiness roaring at me. I so often thought of Fré Cohen letting herself be pushed along, that same wind blowing bushy tangles in her hair so similar to mine. Walking along the beach till she reached that other village on the shore where I was born. Talking a lot, in the company of Max and other like-minded friends maybe, climbing up a steep dune and then, after a coffee break in the rundown café, they would head through the woods to visit their friend Jaap Hemelrijk. And there they would start their discussions all over again, talking into the small hours, sharing dinner with the children, running up and down the stairs, and building a vast and intelligent future for themselves.

But they were Jews.

Never was the push of the wind as rough as that of the policeman who came to arrest Fré. Faster and faster she had moved on her light feet to flee the Nazis, until she stumbled over an informant, some human being somewhere in a remote village in Holland who thought nothing of stopping this gifted creature in her steps. They only thing Fré took with her were suicide pills. Enough to avoid ever facing a death at the hands of the Nazis in 1943. That same year Max was murdered in Sobibor.

It is late in the afternoon. I bring my mug to the kitchen and sit on the swing, my feet aimlessly drawing patterns in the fallen pine needles on the ground. I want my mother to come and pick me up. I go back into the house. He is sitting in his study, smoking a cigar, drinking a glass of jenever and my father is there with him. The two of them are laughing.

When the rowan tree that grows beside his vaulted window, the one at his left hand when he sits at his desk in his study, is heavy with berries, I go to visit him. Straight out of school with some leftover sandwiches in my bag. It is my last day in that school before we move to the South of France. I know he has encouraged my parents to take us there: a new country, a different language to learn. The language of his beloved Marcel Proust. And off they went again talking and talking about people in a book. I can hear them argue in my head when I walk down the garden path. What do I want to learn French for?

He is standing beside the tree, holding out his hands filled with nuts. The birds land on him, confidently.

'See, little Judith, they prefer me to the berries.' He smiles a wide and happy smile. 'You know they share a secret with me that I will tell you one day.' As usual, he takes me with him to another universe. We walk into his study and he tells me to sit down at his desk. He puts his hand on my head in a rabbinical gesture of blessing and we wait for a few minutes in silence. There they come, pecking gently, then louder on the windowpanes of that window similar to a window in a cathedral, the small multicoloured birds are calling their food-man for more, more. He makes me stand under the rowan tree with him, a bag of raw peanuts in my hand. He peels them and feeds his winged friends. I am convinced that he himself will fly off with them in a moment. Then the hour is over and it is getting dark. I kiss his cheeks and climb into my parent's car to drive to another country.

When we come back from living in France I am a teenager and we don't live close to Jaap Hemelrijk anymore. We now talk like adults when the family visits, and I am allowed to read some of the books about World War II. I can read them, but I cannot understand much. During a visit I go looking for something familiar from years back. I wander into the unchanged study and wait for the birds to call at the window. The tree is laden with berries and the birds spread out in a small hungry cloud. We go outside and while he fills the small beaks I ask him why, and what happened to them all, and to him. And what was this secret he shared with these birds? He looks at me with these dark eyes, tells me about the four concentration camps he lived through and how they took him from one camp to the next without bothering to kill him. He was so small, they did not notice him. He has no explanation, he says. He did not hide when they stood in line to go to the gas chambers. They told him to go back to his barracks. He did not need much food like the bigger men, who all died of course. He was strong, but not young and, he laughs and cups his hand to hold a redbreast, he could not fly away. It was a miracle they said, when they found him. No wonder they forgot about you, a rescuing American officer said, look at you Mr Hemelrijk, you are as small as a bird. He bends his head and says he came back, but none of the others did. He says he felt a duty to live. 'Come,' he says, 'these birds need feeding.'

I want to leave school and become a singer, I want to live in music and later I want to write as well. This is what I say to my parents. I am an eager teenager.

On a hot summer afternoon, I stand in my miniskirt – a rose embroidered on my hip, a flower in my massive hair – on the side terrace of the Hemelrijk house. My future, like the future of so many artists that came through this house, is being discussed by the wise people. Because I realize, even as a teenager, that these people have survived something and managed to grow wise.

He tells my parents to let me go and do what I seek to achieve in life: find my freedom. Jaap Hemelrijk was my first real friend ...

BETRAYAL

I FIRST HEARD the name Anne Frank when I was five or six years old, in the house in the dunes. We were sitting in the living room on a quiet afternoon and for some reason I remember that my mother was talking about varnishing the floorboards with a deep purple colour, when the doorbell rang. My father answered the door and brought in a tall and somewhat sombre-looking stranger. I had no idea who he was, but later I was told that it was a man called Otto Frank, who had come all the way from Switzerland to visit us. He went with my father to his study.

Sometime later they emerged, and my father was crying. I had never seen him cry before, so it made a strong and confusing impression on me. Mr Frank had come to visit my father to give him some letters and papers. They related to my father's sister, my aunt Saar. I knew that she had been murdered in a German concentration camp, but my parents rarely talked about these matters, or her, as they thought my sister and I were too young to fully understand the tragedies that had taken place in our family. From the adult's conversation I learned that my aunt Saar had known Mr Frank's daughter Anne in the concentration camp of Auschwitz, before Anne was moved to Bergen-Belsen where she would die months later. Saar was already dead soon after Anne left Auschwitz.

That's how Anne Frank came into my life. It was years later that I read her diary, it was written in my native language, Dutch. But I knew she had been born in Germany, and had come to Holland with her family, fleeing from the Nazi regime. Like many of the Dutch writers and intellectuals of his generation, my father spoke fluent and correct German. Whenever I ventured a sloppy sentence or made a grammatical mistake in the language he worshipped, a tortured frown would appear on his large brow. How painful it must have been, that the clipped language of his family's murderers was the same as the one he had learned to admire and love as an innocent Dutch teenager. We never spoke about it. I read the beautiful leather-bound German books by Heine, Goethe, Schiller and many others in our little black-and-gold painted library. I loved those books with their Gothic script, and I loved the smile on my father's face when he discovered our shared joy in the German language.

When I came to read Anne Frank's diary, I already understood why she had decided to write in Dutch, the language of the country where she was given refuge and grew up, and where eventually, as the world knows, she would go into hiding in an annex behind a house on the Prinsengracht. Then they were betrayed and taken off to Westerbork transit camp, like my aunts and uncles, my grandparents, my cousins, all the members of my family, ranging from toddlers to pensioners. After spending a short period there, they were loaded onto the trains heading east to the extermination camps. None of them ever came back.

After the war, everyone, including my parents, struggled to get back to life as normal, as if that was possible. Only in his very old age did my father open up about those closest to him, who had been betrayed by their fellow citizens and then murdered in the camps. Just like Anne Frank. There has been a lot of research and speculation about the identity of her betrayer. But in Amsterdam there are few secrets.

There was so much unspoken, but everyone knew what had happened. Everyone knew who had betrayed whom. Already as children, we understood that there were shops you didn't set foot in, restaurants you didn't eat in, families you avoided, people you didn't speak to. It was rarely talked about directly, but somehow we knew. Only once, as a child, did I see my father's anger. We were driving past a busy restaurant, one of the best-known in Amsterdam, the owner's name in fat gold letters on the window. And time stood still. I knew, somehow, that these were the people who had told the police about my aunt Saar's hiding place. These people were, evidently, still doing well.

In Amsterdam the traffic is dense and we sit in the car looking at that restaurant. We see eager people in front of their big plates of food. We are all quiet, waiting for the traffic lights to change, the rain to stop, the car to move on. My father's rage comes out of nowhere. He shakes a white-knuckled fist at the over-lit restaurant and shouts through the opened car window: 'Informers!'

MAROR

MY MOTHER'S VOICE was raw and deep when she sang Russian songs or old French ballads. She used to sing everywhere on our adventurous trips. In the streets late at night, in churches where the carved medieval Madonnas and Christs would go *stumm* listening to her passionate renditions of earthy songs. Mother sang like that, with that natural break, that sob in her voice, even when at night she sang our bedtime lullaby. That song I later found in a Tchaikovsky symphony, the way I found my way back to her folk ballads through the classical composers I had the privilege of studying in my teens. The way Stravinsky used to feast on those tunes sung by the peasants of Russia or within the closed Jewish communities and villages, would always bring me back to my mother and her singing. For me it was the singing voice, the voices of people singing at home around me that would be at the start of my life lived with a vocation. We had a radio and a record player that played the music of classical composers for us. Those smooth, highly developed tones from the jubilant sopranos singing Haydn or Mozart held a fatal attraction. I wanted to sing like that – not the way my mother sang.

At a very early age I had a strong voice and the ear to be able to sing along with those trained artists. I decided that I would follow that music with a quasi-religious dedication, and use the colours of my voice to turn singing into the art form I needed to express myself in. I say religious, because I had a belief in that idiom – the one language, the many languages – composers used down the centuries in which I could find my own sound. To develop my own voice, a degree removed from the basic melodies and natural singing styles I needed to study.

The Royal Conservatoire in The Hague took me in as a fifteen-year-old rebel. Much as I was dedicated to both the old and the contemporary masters of classical music, I still wanted it all, the other music, the popular one, the one often considered inferior by my fellow students. I heard the eating and drinking in it and looked for a development in sound through that idiom as well.

My father's smile always broadened when he heard me sing. Yet there was the unspoken understanding that I had to excel. As a singer I had to aim to reproduce the charm and panache of the green violinist in the Chagall painting, in short my voice had to dance and float. There were the great examples, the divas of my time, Callas the artiste and the highly refined Elisabeth Schwarzkopf for example. Her great musical renditions filled my dreams, of becoming a traveller on trains and planes, landing on stages where 'pink' would be my best spotlight, serving the grand masters of classical music while feeding on the breath of multiheaded audiences. I would live off that energy and find that distinctive personal 'timbre' in my voice as I interpreted the works I presented to the world.

As a teenager I sat in the third floor windows of our old canal house in Delft with my legs dangling out over the water, to the background music of velvet voices, avidly reading or very occasionally smoking dope with my friends. In general music and the written word were the drugs I took to survive, to make me feast on the path I had chosen so early in my life.

There were parties and beautiful boys, men playing enchanting music, dragging me into their world of sound. I would believe in their fairy tales for a short while and then wander on, looking for my own story, exploring nature, listening to the wind or living outside time, standing on the ancient bridges of the town, always wanting to sing.

Insatiable nights of music, half-asleep on my mattress on the floor, reaching for the arm of my record player to hear that again and again: the satisfactory scratch of the needle on the record.

My vocal heroines filling my room with their dreams, their sound-stories. I knew I wanted to find them and ask them to hand it to me, their secret – how to sculpt your own voice. They produced sentences from various operas in different languages that stayed glued in my head. They are still there. These were the songlines that would map out my life. Like the Australian Aboriginal people who knew how to recognize their land through songs, I would find the different paths to take through hearing these musical sentences. To me, they were texts filled with meaning.

As a small child I had to attend the Seder, the first night of Pesach, at the house of the very grand and wise Rabbi Meyer. It was a long evening filled with chanting. There was horseradish we had to chew on. It was called *maror*, a bitter herb that symbolised the bitterness of life for the Jews as slaves in Egypt. I remember chewing like a young calf the parsley dipped in salt, to recall the tears (unknown to me then) shed for a difficult life, and subsequently falling asleep on their cosy sofa after having filled my stomach with hard-boiled eggs. Eggs were my favourite food and my childhood was good, so I slept.

I moved to Paris, a penniless twenty-year-old music graduate, carrying my suitcases bulging with dreams.

On my first day there I bought a book of poetry and a red umbrella, for mental and physical shelter. I had my gramophone in my room, and a fierce teacher of French music called Noemie, I had a city full of operatic happenings, there were glamorous shops where they designed diva dresses. The images of the great divas floated forever in my eager mind. I had to reach one to teach me about the mystery of their music-making. As yet, there was little darkness to the beauty of striving for the ultimate perfection in a voice.

The metro stations of Opera and Sèvres-Babylone offered a high, vaulted space for busking in the early evenings when people were going home from work. I chose Monteverdi and Mozart as my money-making companions, and sang for a couple of hours to the passers-by, comfortable in my old boots and torn fur coat. When an agent leaning on a silver-knobbed cane came to listen to me, my busking days were over.

And I entered the world of the diva, Madame Ludwig, who taught me well. She broke me into the real world of classical voices – including my own.

> *Bringing my voice around countless cities, soaking up the scents, the architecture, of different cultures, while remaining strictly confined to my own idiom – classical music. A vast territory to bring across to an appreciative public. Still relying on the expertise of my teachers. Still keeping Elisabeth Schwarzkopf in mind as the ultimate artist, the ultimate teacher …*

By the time I had acquired some performance and interpretative skills – I knew which lighting would enhance my stage appearance and dressed in the glamorous silks that I once drooled over when roaming around the ateliers of Yves Saint Laurent, Paco Rabanne and other grand masters in the fashion industry – I was called up to audition for Schwarzkopf.

One evening in Amsterdam, in a small living room, the stern diva listened to me singing Mozart and decided to take me on for her masterclass. Although, in general, she was quite unkind to the other singers who had been chosen for the masterclass, she was kind and complimentary to me and to my voice. However, she also subjected me to fierce criticism, which I survived.

At the end of the masterclasses there was a grand gala concert in Amsterdam. I introduced my elderly parents to her. She was coldly polite, which was, apparently, her usual manner. When we said goodbye she asked me, strangely enough, if I was really Dutch. The question left me wondering: Why had she asked that? But I was elated by her presence, the fact I had met and worked with her, and that she admired my voice and skills.

One month later, the Salzburg sun shone on the preparations for the music festival that was taking place. I was going to sing and I felt a dangerous boldness in myself. The one that I knew people called happiness, something you had to be wary of I thought. The difficulties in life, the suffering of my family, had become part of me by now. I was ready to chew on the bitter herb.

Elisabeth Schwarzkopf came to greet me backstage, all fur and diamonds, with a carefully lipsticked smile. I was overcome and did not perform well that night. I did not like the Salzburg sun, or Austria, the green collars on the men's jackets, the feathers in their hats. I did love Mozart though.

And then the train took me back to Amsterdam, where I lived with an Irish poet. He was waiting for me at the station. Stepping out of the train I handed him my suitcase and it broke open, its entire contents spilling out over Platform 4. My life was exposed: scores, clothes. I did not care. Somehow I had a premonition that this was the end of an old life, and that a new life was coming down the tracks. The next day someone handed me the book by Alan Jefferson about Elisabeth Schwarzkopf, the voice that had played in my head since the first time I heard her …

I lost mine for a week after I read the book.

1933:   ELISABETH SCHWARZKOPF JOINS THE YOUTH SECTION OF THE NAZI PARTY.

1933:   My grandfather Hijman Mok is cracking jokes, my Aunt Saar is playing Chopin, my father Maurits Mok is writing poems. My mother, Riemke Timmermans, dances the nights away …

1938:   The young, blonde beauty with the silver-toned voice, Ms Schwarzkopf, is a card-carrying member of the Nazi Party, and sings full time at the Deutsche Oper.

1938:   My father and his sister take a walk on the beach, their feet are bare, toes combing through the hot sand. They return to their parents to speak about their worries for the future. Their father laughs in disbelief, such a beautiful evening cannot be spoiled.

1939:   Schwarzkopf becomes acquainted with Joseph Goebbels, Hitler's right hand, Reich Minister of Propaganda. A man with a great sense of culture. He appreciates her art as much as her blonde qualities.

1939:   My mother plans her departure for the USA. Will she ever again see the fields of tulips, the multicoloured blankets that cover her native land?

1940:   Schwarzkopf's German diction is irreproachable, good enough to accept Herr Goebbels' offer to act in Nazi propaganda films. There she plays the racially pure young woman dangling her long legs off a hay stack; Elisabeth Schwarzkopf honours her art.

1940:   The author Maurits Mok publishes his pamphlet expressing his fears about the rise of the ultimate antisemitism; the unspoken fear amongst many music-loving Jews in Holland.

1941–1943:   The years in which her voice is heard by the German rulers, all that counts is musical perfection. Elisabeth Schwarzkopf refines her vocal lines to make Herr Hitler happy – and of course, her cruel lover, the Butcher of Poland, Hans Frank. They hold hands while she recovers from an illness, a pregnancy, fleeting events in the life of the diva – she will prevail.

1941–1943:   My grandparents hold hands, not knowing how to find support. My family wanders through these years: hidden souls, hidden hearts.

1944:   Frau Schwarzkopf performs for the SS – Mozart, Wolf, Schubert, songs that are mine now – songs that she taught me, songs listened to by men who took my grandparents straight to the gas chambers of Auschwitz. Old, useless souls, not even worthy of a tattooed number, the ink was kept to write down the programmes for Ms Schwarzkopf's recitals for the front line troops.

1945:   Freedom and death. Politics are not expressed in song according to some. To Elisabeth Schwarzkopf music is life, music is death.

2006:   Dame Elisabeth Schwarzkopf DBE, Commandeur of the Ordre des Arts et des Lettres, etc., one of the greatest sopranos of the twentieth century and married to a Jewish music producer, the founder of the London Philharmonia, Walter Legge, dies peacefully in Switzerland.

AMSTERDAM

THERE ARE YOUNG children playing in the front garden. One of them is my child, our daughter. A broad waterway flows along the house, its heavy grey reflecting the Dutch sky. Boats and clouds drift by. The hours pass slowly while our hostess prepares the table. Our host returns from playing the violin at a matinee concert with the Concertgebouw Orchestra. His white shirt and undone black dicky-bow hint at another century. We seem to have taken a leap in time again, by agreeing to celebrate the Seder on the first night of Pesach. The food is conventional, but we may not be. We just like to feed our strange nostalgia for a tradition that we have lost. Our children will read from the illustrated Haggadah books and sing songs. And we will make music after we have celebrated the freedom of an enslaved people.

The apricots and nuts taste sweet, the horseradish bitter.

There is the sound of the children's voices, light, high notes that travel from room to room now that they have escaped the drill of the evening, the eggs and matzoh, the intense questions about Egypt they were expected to have an answer for.

I remain sitting alone at the empty table with the leftovers of biblical foods strewn around on the white tablecloth. Mostly when I am alone, I can hear a song or a melody shaping up in my head. It is not a Sephardic or Yiddish tune that I hear, it is the voice of Elisabeth Schwarzkopf pulling me along by a silver thread, making me sink into a different kind of nostalgia than the one this evening has brought on. The sadness of accepting who she was. And then I realize that I have tasted it: the bitter herb of life. Her voice, her betrayal.

She is my *maror*.

DUBLIN 2017

WITH THE PHONE still in my hand I try to imagine an early spring, in a house in the well-to-do neighbourhood of Bilthoven, a small town in the wooded centre of Holland. The house was owned by an idealistic family who had set up their own school and, when the war started, thought it only logical to help hide people who were being threatened with extermination, among them Jews. My grandparents were living in this house. My aunt visited them.

Holland is a stolid country, where daily life changes very little. I imagine my family sitting in a spacious living room on an afternoon in late March, 1944. The tall trees in the garden are sprouting and a bleak sun shines through the bay windows, enough to light up the harmonious green and brown old Dutch interior. My grandfather is reading one of his favourite novels, my grandmother is mending the clothes, worn out by now, that they have been able to bring with them from home. My aunt Saar is out. Her fake papers are working well enough for her to be able to visit her friends and play the piano. She joins them to play chamber music at least twice a week; she wants to keep her fingers supple. Now she is on her way back to the house, maybe humming a phrase from Schubert's 'Die Forelle'. Schubert and Chopin remain her favourite composers. Her feet hurt, so she hums louder. I know that the soles of her shoes were so thin she can feel the ground with her toes. My grandmother suffers the least; she likes to wear slippers all the time. Anyway, she can't leave the house. She is a Jew and she has been served the official German papers ordering her to leave her house and join other Jews to be deported to a concentration camp. This afternoon, she is not thinking about those papers. The house is warm and she dozes into a dream over her needlework. Her hands still holding the dress that she is mending, she remembers the fine fabrics her father used.

The click of his scissors when he cut into the fabric with utter precision. A regular clicking and then the tear of the fabric. A short cough. The flutter of fine pattern paper. He is holding up the paper shadow of a customer's new coat. She sits on the floor surrounded by scraps and rags and makes this and that, shifting around the colours. The smell of new clothes is overwhelming. No human sweat or stain has impregnated these coats and dresses yet. My grandmother likes things to be clean, very clean. Now she smiles, thinking of the drone of her father's voice when he lets the butterflies out in his favourite story about the silk spinners.

'Tea?' My grandfather gets up and suggests a brew that they like to pretend is tea. She wakes up out of her daydream, still hoping that it is their maid, from way back then, who will bring in tea and that the customer will come about his coat. She tells my grandfather about her dreams of the past and what an excellent tailor her father was. He nods in agreement for the umpteenth time: he has been hearing this comment from her since they were married. 'And that he was ...'

Was it the feeling of ordinariness, the old couple's stale conversation, the promise of spring in the light, the thickness of the thoughts in the novel he was reading that he needed to get through on his own – all of these things maybe – that made him decide to put on his coat and hat and go outside into the world that was forbidden to him?

Their daughter, my aunt, walks slowly. Past the woods, past the small flowers covering the ground, past the peaceful silence. She feels nervous, can't remember where she left the letter she wrote to her partner Leo, who is in hiding with her back in the capital, Amsterdam. They do that sometimes. Write letters to each other, as if to pretend that they still travel and are busy with work, instead of being in this prison that is their actual life.

He knows she has to visit her family now and then. And that she is relatively safe with her fake *Ausweis*, her identity card.

He, Leo, draws on everything he can find, talks about finding his famous friend in Amsterdam. He knows Max is here, but is not sure if he can trust him. All his old buddies have told him that Max Beckmann is an apolitical man with one focus in life: painting. Of course his work has been burnt by the Nazis as *Entartete Kunst*, degenerate art, and he had to flee Germany, but he is still a German goy and does not run too many risks. How good it would be to have a conversation with him about work and get the rattle of the Nazi trucks out of his head for a while; to talk about their mutual friends, talk about Berlin, Germany, back in the days of art and their productive madness. Leo's sons came with him on the train when they left Berlin for Amsterdam, where he went to live with my musical aunt. They went to live elsewhere. He worries about his children as well. Where are they?

My aunt stuffs her hands in her pockets, it is getting chilly. Her coat is a gift and looks new. Ah, the letter is actually in the pocket of her coat. She will not stay tonight. She decides to go back to Amsterdam instead. The trains are running perfectly. Holland is running smoothly, on track and on time. She can hear her wooden heels click on the pavement. A true sign of decadence, my grandmother remarked. Heels were supposed to be made of leather. My aunt smiles at the thought and starts to walk faster. There is that little girl, my half-sister, she wants to see before she leaves ...

My grandfather walks past the stately houses, his small frame bent, his eyes on the ground, breathing in the air of freedom for a couple of minutes, furtively. Angrily as well, they have not turned him into an animal yet. Their eyes are on him though: a neighbour stands in the window and watches the old Jew walking past his house. Picks up the phone and calls the police. He had suspected those modernistic neighbours of his were hiding Jews. Well, that was that, they'd be gone soon.

'Yes, good afternoon, is this police headquarters? A small matter I would like to mention to you: there are Jews in hiding at my neighbour's house.'

How well I can imagine the perfectly polite voice on the phone sending my family to their deaths.

My grandfather doesn't notice him. He looks at his watch and thinks he should go back to safety. He strokes his watch mechanically. He was so proud of it. It is the watch from the City of Amsterdam that he won in a spelling competition when he was sixteen. Uneducated Hijman, who left school at twelve and always hungered for knowledge. Hijman, who liked to tell endless jokes. In every job situation that he landed himself in and out of, he was the joker. At least his son Mozes, my father, who for some reason when he grew up changed his name to Maurits, seems to have abandoned all plans to have a normal job, a normal life. He would like to see his son. His son, who refuses to wear the obligatory yellow *Jude* star on his clothes, and mixes with famous authors and artists. Twenty-six times they reprinted his long poem. His son is a success and famous. He nearly smiles when he reaches the front door. He just wishes his son wouldn't be so dramatic about their future. Not that he is prepared to go to one of these work camps in Germany or Poland and work for the bastards. But surely things are not as bad as Mozes keeps telling them. He shakes his head and turns the key in the well-polished door.

My grandmother is brushing the little girl's hair and scolding her about stuff she did not pick off the floor, and so on and so on ... When my grandfather comes into the living room, he strokes her hair and starts telling her a funny story about a squirrel he saw gnawing on a German soldier's cap that was lying underneath a bush. Imagine ...

The doorbell rings. A stifling feeling of panic takes hold of them as they push the little girl, my half-sister, into the space between the double walls, a hiding place, and tell her to keep very, very quiet. She does, and she presses her ear to the wall so she can hear what's going on. She hears the owners of the house running down the stairs and opening the front door. She hears the polite, curt greetings of the police and how they walk into the living room to find the old people. Nothing much is said except, get your coats, take your bags. The front door opens again and my aunt Saar walks in. Questions are asked. The owners tell the police that she is a friend of the family and then suddenly, my confused grandmother tells the police that she is her daughter. And so Saar is taken with them.

The three of them write one letter from jail. It is addressed to the little girl who is now in hiding somewhere else, the girl who waved a silent, last, goodbye at them through a wall.

'We are healthy and well, little one, we will see you soon,' the letter says.

The people that have been hiding my family are arrested as well.

It is the end of March 1944; my grandparents and my aunt have been separated and my aunt is brought to Amsterdam to be held in a theatre. They had a good piano in there somebody told me, and the acoustics were good as well. Did she sit in the front row one night of the fourteen she spent there, thinking: I am still alive, I am here, and I can play. Her scores were left in Bilthoven. I can see her name on them now, in firm handwriting. Years later, I got these scores. When I started playing Chopin, my father would stand in the room listening for someone to come back, to come home.

There were a lot of children in that theatre, the Hollandsche Schouwburg. My aunt Saar played with them, played for them, shared whatever food she had and told them many stories until they left in trucks for Westerbork transit camp.

How often did I walk past that theatre in its leafy neighbourhood, the zoo close by, the house of the chief rabbi of Amsterdam around the corner. Close, very close to the house my aunt had shared with her partner Leo, who was also betrayed and arrested and deported.

That theatre is a wall with names on it now, one of them is my aunt's name: Saar Mok.

My sister.

It was her. She just told me on the phone that she was there. Hidden in between the two walls, they somehow forgot about her, the little girl, the child. How the guilt of not being with them had strangled her for an entire lifetime. How she heard them go and could not say goodbye. How she could never tell us, her sisters, that she heard them. Go.

Leabharlanna Poiblí Chathair Baile Átha Cliath
Dublin City Public Libraries